Known
Military Dead
during
War *of* 1812

Dedicated *to the* Unknown Soldiers *and* Sailors *who died during*

The War *of* 1812

Compiled by:
Ex-Lieut. Clarence Stewart Peterson

Southern Historical Press, Inc.
Greenville, South Carolina

This volume was reproduced
from a personal copy located in
the Publishers private library

Please direct all correspondence and book orders to:
SOUTHERN HISTORICAL PRESS, Inc.
PO Box 1267
Greenville, SC   29602-1267

CLARENCE STEWART PETERSON

———

Author of:

Bibliography of County Histories of The 2980 Counties in The 48 States	1935
Governors Lists of The 48 States	1938
The American Pioneer in 48 States	1944
Bibliography of County Histories of The 3050 Counties In The 48 States, 1st Rev. Ed.	1944
Teaching 48 States Histories by Counties	1945
Admiral John A. Dahlgren	1945
America's Rune Stone	1946
Bibliography of County Histories of The 3111 Counties in The 48 States, 2nd Rev. Ed.....................................	1946
First Governors of the 48 States (Set in Braille by Library of Congress)	1947
Governors Lists of The 48 States, 1st Rev. Ed.	1947
American-Scandinavian Diplomatic Relations 1776-1876	1948
Red River Valley Territorial Pioneers	1949
St. Croix River Valley Territorial Pioneers	1949
International Boundary Territorial Pioneers	1949
Meeker County Territorial Pioneers...........................	1949
Stephen Taylor 1757-1857, Only Revolutionary Soldier Buried in Minnesota..............	1949
Swift County's First Pioneers	1949
Supplement to Bibliography of County Histories................	1950
Last Civil War Veteran in Each State.........................	1951
Known Descendants of Carl Olofsson Born in Sweden - 1685 to 1954......................................	1953
Known Military Dead During the War of 1812	1955
1955 Supplement to Bibliography of County Histories In U. S. ..	1955

FOREWORD

Dear Mr. Peterson:

I am glad to be informed of the good work you are doing in listing these people who gave patriotic service to our state and nation.

The sacrifice of these men was one of the things which made it possible for later generations to develop our new land along the principles established by the patriots of the Revolution.

The War of 1812 established our new nation as a going concern and showed the other nations of the world we had a stable government. The patriots who served in that war were one of the generations of men who were called upon for the supreme sacrifice in order that future generations might enjoy the blessings of liberty and the heritage of individual freedom and opportunity.

Sincerely yours,

J. B. Johnson,

Governor of Vermont

Dear Mr. Peterson:

Thank you for your interesting copyrighted picture of the last veterans of the Revolutionary War, War of 1812, and Mexican War.

Permit me to congratulate you on the excellent work you are doing in preserving important information concerning the records of the known military dead, particularly in reference to your forthcoming volume relating to the War of 1812.

Please call on me at any time we can serve you with any information about Georgia historical matters.

Sincerely,

Marvin Griffin,

Governor of Georgia

FOREWORD (continued)

EXECUTIVE DEPARTMENT

Annapolis, Maryland

May 5, 1955

Mr. Clarence Stewart Peterson
Baltimore 3, Maryland

Dear Mr. Peterson:

Following is brief foreword to your "Known Military Dead During

the War of 1812":

Research into statistics and the compiling of lists
are tedious tasks, but they are essential to the detail
and accuracy of history.

Orators and writers, both of prose and poetry, need,
at times, the statistics and the lists. They are valuable
for students and often necessary to the work of essayists.

Frequently such compilations are the important family
links that figure prominently in the settling of estates,
the obtaining of birth certificates, the location of lost
relatives, and many other occurrences in the lives of a
community, a State or a Nation.

It is fortunate, then, that the minds of some few
among us turn with determination and even with enjoyment
to that which most of us seek to avoid - the compiling of
the valuable and useful lists.

Clarence Stewart Peterson is such a compiler. This,
his latest work - "Known Military Dead During the War of 1812"--
is a work that required very extensive research and time
consuming inquiry. Like many of his earlier productions it
is a worthy and admirable addition to the Nation's History.

Sincerely,

Theodore R. McKeldin

Governor

STATE OF OHIO

ADJUTANT GENERAL'S DEPARTMENT

COLUMBUS 16

4 May 1955

THE WAR OF 1812

      Because of war having been declared, President Madison issued instructions to Governor Return Jonathan Meigs of Ohio, in April 6, 1812, to assemble the Militia at Dayton, Ohio, to be drilled and prepared to march to Detroit.

      By the end of the month more than the required number of men had been enrolled.

      Early in May these troops were fairly equipped and had chosen their Field Officers. The President had commissioned Governor Hull of Michigan, as Brigadier General. General Hull arrived at Dayton, Ohio, on May 25, 1812, and left with his troops, June 1.

      According to records in the Adjutant General's Department at Columbus, Ohio furnished for this war 1759 officers and 24,521 enlisted men distributed as follows:

         First Regiment Infantry, 108 Companies
         Second Regiment Infantry, 85 Companies
         Third Regiment Infantry,   56 Companies
         Unassigned Infantry, 185 Companies
         Assigned to U. S. Infantry, 5 Companies
         Mounted Infantry, 25 Companies
         Cavalry, 13 Troops
         Artillery, 1 Battery

      The above units and the men composing these units served with distinction during the War of 1812.

            For the Governor of the State of Ohio
                Frank J. Lausche

           By: Major General Leo M. Kreber
                Adjutant General of Ohio

COMMONWEALTH OF KENTUCKY

Executive Chamber

Frankfort

April 18, 1955

Mr. Clarence S. Peterson
Box 342
Baltimore, Maryland

Dear Mr. Peterson:

The War of 1812 was the first conflict in which Kentucky as a State contributed its sons to the American Army. The hundreds of Kentuckians who fought in this war reveal the patriotism they felt for America, a noble characteristic that remains with all Kentuckians today.

With kind regards, I am

Sincerely yours,

Lawrence W. Wetherby

Governor

ACKNOWLEDGMENTS AND BIBLIOGRAPHY

In the preparation of "Known Military Dead During The War of 1812", special acknowledgment and thanks is due President National Mrs. Frederic G. Bauer, Ridgewood, New Jersey, and Mrs. C. F. Quillian, Librarian-Secretary, National Headquarters, 1461 Rhode Island Avenue, N. W., Washington, D. C., National Society, U. S. Daughters of 1812; the staffs in the National Archives, War Records Sections, Washington, D. C.; the Chiefs of Military History, Department of Defense; and the staff of the Library of Congress.

Special acknowledgment and thanks is due the state officers of the N. S. U. S. Daughters of 1812 and Mrs. Alice Zurner Miller, a former official of this organization, for the generous aid given the author; the adjutant generals of the United States and of the eighteen states that fought the war of 1812; the state and local historical societies and libraries of these eighteen states; the Society of The War of 1812; the national and state officials of military parks and monuments in these eighteen states; and all aid given by colonial and patriotic organizations, public and private.

The War of 1812 was fought by eighteen states - the original thirteen states that formed the Union, and the following five, with date they joined the Union: Vermont, 1791; Kentucky, 1792; Tennessee, 1796; Ohio, 1803; and Louisiana, 1812.

The military forces on land and sea of these eighteen states in the Union fought several battles at sea and eighty-six skirmishes, engagements, affairs, sorties, and battles on land, resulting in casualities in Michigan, Illinois, Georgia, Upper and Lower Canada, Ohio, New York, Virginia, Alabama, Wisconsin, Maryland, Washington, D.C., Florida and Louisiana, as found listed in the records in the office of the United States Adjutant General in Washington, D. C., which are now on deposit in the National Archives, Washington, D. C.

The History of The Medical Department of The U. S. Navy in World War II, published by the U. S. Government Printing Office, Washington, D. C., states that the United States Navy and Marine Corps casualties in the War of 1812 totaled 815; for Navy, 265 killed and 439 wounded, and for the Marine Corps, 45 killed and 66 wounded.

The vessels in the U. S. Navy in 1812 before the war with Great Britain were the following, (the underscored were lost in the war, the Boston was badly burnt at Washington and not worth repairs, as was also the New York which escaped flames): United States, President, Constitution, Chesapeake, Constellation, Congress, New York, Adams, Boston, Essex, John Adams, Louisiana, Hornet, Wasp, Adams, Oneida, Syren, Argus, Enterprize, Rattlesnake, Nautilus, Vixen, Viper, schooner Vixen, besides gun-boats, bombs, etc., according to The Naval Monument by A. Bowen.

Heitman's Historical Register and Dictionary of the U. S. Army, Vol. 2, p. 295, states that in the War of 1812 the Regular Army had 72 engagements which resulted in 65 officers and 1235 enlisted men killed;

B

on p. 281 he states that in this war not over 60,000 Regulars were engaged and 31,210 officers and 440,412 men, totalling 471,622 who served with the militia and volunteers of which 577 were killed.

The War of 1812 was declared on June 18, 1812. The Treaty of Peace ending that war was signed at Ghent, Belgium, December 24, 1814 and was ratified by Congress February 17, 1815.

Volume 5 Dictionary of American History states that United States deaths in the War of 1812 totaled 1877. This number is questionable. For instance, the Battle of Plattsburgh, unique because it was an engagement waged on land and sea, deserved to rank as one of the decisive battles of the world. Exactly what the losses of the land battle at Plattsburg were is not known. Prevost's dead, wounded and deserted have been placed as low as 235 and as high as 2500, while Macomb's casualties have been estimated to be under 100. In the naval battle Macdonough reported 52 killed and 58 wounded. The British reported 57 killed and 72 wounded.

Charles J. Ingersoll in "Historical Sketch of The Second War Between The United States of America and Great Britain" states on page 182, quoted from report of British General Ross: "On taking possession of the city, we also set fire to the President's palace, the Treasury, and the War office." On page 183: "But unfortunately, it did not stop here; a noble library, several printing offices, and all the national archives were likewise committed to the flames, which, though no doubt the property of government, might better have been spared." Further on page 183: "That the complete destruction of even only public buildings, officially reported by the commanding admiral and general to their government, was the object of the expedition, is of authentic and undeniable record."

"At the time of the burning of Washington by the British on August 24, 1814, the historically valuable records were destroyed," from Preface of General Entry Book of American Prisoners of War at Quebec, by Mrs. Henry James Carr.

In the War of 1812 "served some of the most magnificent men in American history - James Lawrence of the Chesapeake, Oliver Perry at Lake Erie, Thomas Macdonough at Lake Champlain, Andrew Jackson at New Orleans, and Joshua Barney at Bladensburg" - from "Poltroons and Patriots".

K. C. Babcock states in his "The Rise of American Nationality", p.188: "The most liberal estimate of loss of men, in battles on sea and land, in camp, in hospital, and in prisons, places it at 30,000 men. Some 1500 killed, 5000 killed and wounded, 9700 killed wounded and prisoners". Many Indians in service were killed whose names are not given, so no complete list will ever be made of those who died during the War of 1812.

In this research, splendid assistance was given the author on personal visits by the staffs of the Bridgeport, Connecticut Public Library; New York Historical Society Reference Library, the New York Public Library, and Columbia University Library, New York City; Newark City Library and New Jersey State Historical Society Library, Newark, New Jersey; Philadelphia City Library and Penn State Historical Society Library, Philadelphia, Pa.;

Delaware Archives, Wilmington, Delaware; Johns Hopkins University Library, Peabody Library, and the Enoch Pratt Free Library, Baltimore, Maryland; Library of Congress, National Archives, U. S. Defense Department Libraries, and the National Library of the National Society U. S. Daughters of 1812 in Washington, D. C.; the Richmond City Library and the Virginia State Historical Society Library, Richmond, Virginia.

A list follows which is a brief bibliography of some of the most important source material and references used in this research. Numerous histories dealing with the War of 1812 are available and many of them were used, but the mention of them are here omitted. Much valuable aid was received from the following records and works: General Entry Book of American Prisoners of War at Quebec, Vols. I and II, compiled by Mrs. Henry James Carr under the auspices of the National Society U. S. Daughters of 1812.

Military Note Book #135 (570) Deaths, Discharges & Substitutes 1815 to 1823.

Index to Grave Records of Soldiers of War of 1812 Buried In Ohio, by U. S. Daughters of War of 1812.

Barkhamsted Men In War of 1812. By Wm. W. Lee, Meriden, Conn.

Military Records of Schoharie County Veterans, New York. Compiled by George H. Warner, Henry Parslow, Henry Letcher.

Rolls of Mississippi Commands In War of 1812, pub. by Mississippi Historical Society.

Summary of The Proceedings of Congress Including a Collection of All the State Papers and Official Documents Published During the Interesting Period of The War of 1812.

History of The Medical Department of The U. S. Navy in World War II.

Historical Register and Dictionary of U. S. Army From Its Origin, Sept. 29, 1789 to March 2, 1903, Vols. I & II. By Francis B. Heitman, Government Printing Office, Washington, D.C.

Historical Register of The United States, 1812-14, Palmer, T. H. - Phila. 1916.

Returns of the Killed and Wounded of American Troops in Battles - Or Engagements with Indians, British or Mexican Troops From the Year 1790, to the Close of The War With Mexico, in 1848. Compiled by Lieut. Col. J. H. Eaton, 3rd Infantry 1850-1.

Record of Bounty Land Relinquished for Five Years Pension Under Act of April 16, 1816.

Lossing, Benson J. - The Pictorial Field - Book of The War of 1812, N. Y. Harpers, 1869.

List of Pensioners of The War of 1812, edited by Byron N. Clark, published by Research Pub. Co., Boston, 1904.

#576 Hospital Returns 1814-15.
Williamsville Hospital Returns #147
Williamsville Hospital Returns #148

Book #34 (552) Northern Army; Hospital Records 1814.

Book #135 - Casualties U. S. Army, 1815-23.

American State Papers, Naval Affairs, Vol. I, 1794-1825.

Historical Sketch of The Second War Between The United States of America and Great Britain Declared by Act of Congress the 18th of June 1812 and concluded by Peace, the 15th of February 1815. By Charles J. Ingersoll, Phila. Lea & Blanchard 1849.

Niles Weekly Register.

American State Papers, Vol. 16; Military Affairs, Vol. 1 #123 - 1813.

Grave Records of 1812 in Ohio. By N. S. U. S. Daughters of 1812.

Official Letters of The Military and Naval Officers of the U. S. During the War With Britain 1812-1815. By John Brannan.

Official Accounts, In Detail, of All the Battles Fought by Sea and Land, Between the Navy and Army of The United States, and the Navy and Army of Great Britain 1812, 13, 14 & 15. By H. A. Fay, Late Capt. in the Corps of U. S. Artillerists, N. Y. Printed by E. Conrad 1817.

List of Officers of the U. S. Navy and Marine Corps From 1775 to 1900, Including Regular and Volunteer Corps.

Complete Army & Navy Register of The U. S. 1776- 1887, Part 2, by Ed. Hamersly.

Register of Officer Personnel, U. S. Navy & Marine Corps and Ships Data 1801-1807.

Dictionary of All Officers in The Army of The U. S., including officers of the Navy who have served with the land forces 1789-1853. By Gardner, C. K.

Military Heroes of War of 1812, by Charles J. Peterson.

Those Killed and Wounded, Sept. 13, 1814 at Fort McHenry, Patriotic Marylander I, Sept. 1914, 41-2.

U. S. House of Rep. Misc. Reports, 21st Congress, 1st Session, Feb. 1, 1830. Report #144.

The Ohio Country 1783-1815 Military Operations. Slocum, Charles E.

Soldiers of War of 1812 From Franklin County, Ohio, by Franklin County Pioneer Assn.

Delaware Archives Lists for Militia in War of 1812.

Pennsylvania Archives Lists for Militia in War of 1812.

Lineage Book 1895-1929 for Pennsylvania, compiled by Mrs. Henry James Carr. Pub. by Westmoreland Chapter, Natl. Soc. U. S. Daughters of 1812, Scranton.

Roster Maryland State Society U. S. Daughters of 1812.

National Society U. S. Daughters of 1812 News Letter.

A Journal of a Young Man of Massachusetts at Dartmoor Prison England.
By Benjamin Waterhouse, Boston, 1816.

Benjamin F. Palmer's Privateersman Diary as Prisoner on English War Ships,
at Melville Island and Dartmoor, England.

A Prisoner's Memoirs Or Dartmoor Prison. By C. Andrews, N. Y. 1852.

Journal of Joseph Valpey, Jr., of Salem, Nov. 1813 - April 1815 With Other
Papers Relating to His Experiences In Dartmoor Prison. Pub. by
Mich. Society of Colonial Wars 1922 - Giving American Prisoners
Who Died in the Hospital at Dartmoor, England.

Book 137 Deaths Retired Enlisted Men 1809-1819.

U. S. Pension List of 1820.

The British Invasion of Maryland 1812-15. By William M. Marine.

Historical Sketch of Second War Between U. S. & Britain, by Chas. J. Ingersoll.

The Rise of American Nationality, by K. C. Babcock.

Record of Service of Connecticut Men In The War of The Revolution, War of
1812, Mexican War, by Conn. Adjutant General's Office, Hartford,
Conn., 1889.

Index of Wills Office of Secretary of State of N. J. 1804-1830, by
N. J. Secretary of State's Office.

Records of Officers and Men of New Jersey In Wars 1791-1815, Compiled
by Office of N. J. Adjutant General.

History of U. S. Army. 2 Vols.

Index to Documents of The State of New Jersey 1789-1904.
By Adelaide R. Hasse, N. Y. Pub. Library.

Minutes of Votes and Proceedings of The One Hundredth General Assembly of
The State of New Jersey, Assembly Chamber, Trenton, N.J. Jan. 11, 1876.

Index to Geneological Periodicals, by D. K. Jacobus, Vol. II, New Haven,
Connecticut, 1948.

An Index of The Source Records of Maryland Geneological, Biographical,
Historical, by Mrs. Edward Boteler Passano.

N. Y. Society of The War of 1812 Proceedings 1910-25.

Convention Proceedings of The Veterans and Societies of The War of 1812.

List of Pensioners of The U. S. Pension Roll, Jan. 1, 1883 - U.S. Gov't. Pub.

Kentucky Soldiers In War of 1812 - Report by Ky. Adj. General, Frankfort.

Historical Register of The U. S. By T. H. Palmer.

The Naval Monument On All Naval Battles Between U. S. and Britain and
Algiers, by A. Bowen, Boston, 1840.

A List of Pensioners of The War of 1812, by Byron N. Clark.

Collection of Official Accounts War of 1812, Herman Allen Fay.

Dictionary of American History.

U. S. Army Almanac.

Lancaster County, Penn. Historical Society Military Records.

Index to Certified Copy of List of American Prisoners of War 1812-15,
   compiled by Mrs. Henry James Carr.

Grave Survey of Mich. Veterans of War of 1812. By Mrs. Alice Turner Miller.

Soldiers of The War of 1812 in Ohio. Compiled by N.S.U.S. Daughters of 1812.
   "   " "   "   "   "   " Wisconsin. "   "   " "   "   " "
   "   " "   "   "   "   " Pennsylvania"   "   " "   "   " "

Niagara Frontier, Details, 1814 - Book No. 32 (452)

Northern Army, Hospital Records, 1814 - Book No. 34 (552)

Register Casualties and Daily Occurrencies, 1813. Book No. 28

Register A.G.O. 1814 - Book No. 31 (126)

Substitutes, Deaths, Discharges, 1815-1823 - Book No. 135 (570)

Williamsville Hospital Register, 1814 - Book No. 147 (630)

Williamsville Hospital Check List Entry #71, 1814-1815; Book No. 148 (683)

Casualties and Daily Occurrencies, Register of Northern Army, 1813-
   Book No. 28.

Deaths, Discharges and Substitutes 1815 to 1823 - Book No. 135 (570)

Deaths, Fourth Military District, 1813-1814, Book No. 18 (95)

Deaths, Retired Enlisted Men 1809 to 1819 - Book No, 137
Discharges 1815 to 1816 - Book No. 134 (568)
Deaths and Substitutes 1815 to 1823 - Book No. 135 (570)

Discharges, Greenbush Cantonment 1814-1816 Northern Army--Book No.131 (550)
Discharges - Plattsburg 1812-1815-- Book #132 (562)
Discharges - Sockett Harbor 1814-1815 — Book #133 (561)
Hospital Records, Northern Army, 1814 - Book No. 34 (552)

Lyons Creek (near Ft. Erie) Upper Canada, engagement Oct. 19 & 20, 1814.
   Book No. 33 (456)

Maryland Armory Book 1813-1820 — Book No. 165

Grave Locations of 266 Service Men In War of 1812. Buried in Maine in 1955.
   Compiled by Mrs. Daniel H. Sheehan, Pres. Maine Society, U.S.D. 1812
   and Mrs. Basil I. Lamb, Pres. Preble Chap. U.S.D. 1812, Portland.

                              Ex-Lieut. Clarence Stewart Peterson, M.A.

Washington's Birthday
   February 22, 1955
Baltimore, Maryland

KNOWN MILITARY DEAD DURING THE WAR OF 1812

Name	Rank	Unit		Date	Location
Abbet, Samuel	Sailor	From Mass.	Died	2-28-14	At Chatham
Abbot, Daniel L.	Private	4th Inf.	"	3-13-14	
Abbott, George	"	33rd Inf.	"	10-13-14	
Abbott, John	"	11th Inf.	"	4-13-13	
Abers, Silas	"	15th Inf.	"	7-30-14	
Absolom, Thomas	"	16th Inf.	"	7-7-13	
Ackerman,	Sailor	On Surprise	"	4-15-15	
Ackleman, Jacob	Private	12th Inf.	"	6-19-14	
Adair, William	"	2nd Art.	"	4-6-13	
Adam, John	Sailor	Champlain Sqd.	Killed	9-11-14	
Adams, Eber	Private	23rd Inf.	Died	1-24-15	
Adams, James	"	2nd Art.	"	1-19-15	
Adams, James H.	"	2nd Art.	"	6-20-13	
Adams, John		From Wash. D.C.	"	11-6-14	Dartmoor Prison
Adams, John	Sailor	From N. Y.	"	3-31-14	At Chatham
Adams, John	"	From South Carolina	"	11-6-13	Dartmoor Prison
Adams, John	"	From North Carolina	"	12-3-14	" "
Adams, John	"	Essex	Killed	3-28-14	
Adams, Joseph	"	Constitution	"	12-29-12	
Adams, Long	Private	Ky. Mil.	Died	6-17-13	
Adams, Luther	"	25th Inf.	"		
Adams, Robert	Sailor	From Mass.	"	2-5-15	Dartmoor Prison
Adams, Samuel	Officer		"	11-19-14	
Adams, William	Private	9th Inf.	"	Sept.1813	
Adams, William		From Conn.	"	3-15-15	
Addams, Thomas	Private	15th Inf.	"	6-29-12	
Adigo, Henry	Sailor	From Pa. on Argus	"	1813	Dartmoor Prison
Adms, Lewis	Private	25th Inf.	"	7-18-13	
Aisquith, Edward	Captain	1st Rifles	"	Apr.1815	
Albert, Jacob	Captain		"	1814	
Alden, Samuel	Private	40th Inf.	"	6-5-14	
Aldridge, Israel	"	45th Inf.	"	9-15-14	
Alese, Stewart	"	Ky. Inf.	"	10-31-14	
Alexander, Benj.	"	17th Inf.	"	1-10-15	
Alexander, Charles	"	2nd Art.	"	1-18-15	
Alexander, John	"	Ky. Mil.	"	12-6-10	
Alexander, William	Lieut.	Ky. Mil.	"	2-3-15	
Allen,	Captain	Argus	"	3-15-15	Dartmoor Prison
Allen, Andrew	Private	41st Inf.	"	--	
Allen, Archibald		From N. J.	"	3-4-15	Dartmoor Prison
Allen, Asy		From Mass.	"	11-14-14	" "
Allen, Daniel		42nd Inf.	"	--	
Allen, David O.	Private	25th Inf.	"	--	
Allen, James W.	Sailor	Lawrence	Killed	12-31-13	
Allen, John	Colonel	Constitution	"		
Allen, John	"	1 Reg. Ky. Rifles	"	1-22-13	River Raisin
Allen, John		From N. Y.	Died	11-21-14	Dartmoor Prison
Allen, Jr. John	Private	21st Inf.	"	8-6-13	
Allen, John		From N.Y. on Herald	"	1813-14	Dartmoor Prison
Allen, John B.	Sailor	" "	"	11-21-13	" "
Allen, John D.	"	Constitution	Killed	12-29-12	

Name	Rank	Unit	Fate	Date	Location
Allen, Joseph	Private	4th Rifles	Died	12-11-19	
Allen, Peter	Sailor	Essex	Killed	3-28-14	
Allen, Noah	Corporal	9th Inf.	Died	11-1-14	
Allen, Silas	Private	15th Inf.	"	Feb.1913	
Allen, Silas	"	30th Inf.	"	10-5-14	
Allen, William	Sailor	From R.I.	"	2-19-14	At Chatham
Allen, Wm. H.	Captain	Argus	Killed	8-14-13	
Alley, Peter	Private	41st Inf.	Died	2-14-14	
Allice, Henry	Private	--	"	2-14-14	
Alligo, Henry	Sailor	New York	"	12-23-13	Dartmoor Prison
Allis, Henry	Private	16th Inf.	"	2-4-13	
Allison			Killed		Gasport Navy Yard
Allison	Mate	U.S. Boat #139	Died	1-15-14	
Allison, Robert	Ensign		Killed	8-5-12	
Alloway, Joshua	Private		Died	--	
Alvord, Elisha	Private	11th Inf.	"	11-11-14	
Ambrose, Alamond	Sailor	From N.Y.	"	10-24-13	Dartmoor Prison
Ames, Josiah	Private	23rd Inf.	"	7-29-14	
Amling, Ezra	"	--	"	6-3-13	Quebec Prison
Ammon, Saul	"	15th Inf.	"	--	
Amos, Alamanga	Sailor	Carthegina	"	9-24-14	Dartmoor Prison
Amos, Gaines	Private	35th Inf.	"	2-1-15	
Amos, Peter	Sailor	From Mass. on Napoleon	"	1813	Dartmoor Prison
Amos, Peter	Sailor	From Mass. on Napoleon	"	2-18-15	Dartmoor Prison
Anderson,	Colonel	--	Killed	1-9-15	
Anderson, Alexander		New York	Died	12-29-14	Dartmoor Prison
Anderson, Eli	Private	4th Inf.Va.Mil.	"	Sept.1814	
Anderson, Isaac	Sailor	N.H.	"	12-25-14	Dartmoor Prison
Anderson, James	"	Essex	Killed	3-28-14	
Anderson, Jacob	"	N.H.	Died	1-27-13	Dartmoor Prison
Anderson, John	Colonel	Tenn.Mil.	"	10-27-14	
Andre, Gregorius	1 Lieut.		Killed	9-12-14	
Andre, Gregorius	" "		"	7-24-13	
Andrews, Joseph	Sailor	Mass.	Died	1-4-13	At Chatham
Andrews, Joshua	"	"	"	12-23-14	Dartmoor Prison
Andrews, Josiah	"	"	"	11-22-14	" "
Angel, Michael	Private	Dragoons	"	--	
Annety, John	"	6th Inf.	"	--	
Annis, William	"	45th Inf.	"	3-5-15	
Anthony, Samuel	Corporal	Ky.Mil.	"	9-28-13	
Anthony, William B.		Tenn.Vol.Cav.	Killed	12-28-14	
Anwright, Thos.	Sailor	Champ.Sqd.	"	9-11-14	
Applegate, Elisha	Private	Ky.Mil.	Died	1-7-15	
Appleton, Daniel	Sailor	Mass.Frolic	"	1814	Dartmoor Prison
Appleton, Daniel	"	N.H.	"	1-4-15	" "
Arbuccle, John	Private	-	"	-	
Archer, Daniel	Sailor	Mass.	"	1-26-14	Dartmoor Prison
Archibald, Wm.	Private	Ky.Mil.	"	7-1-13	
Armisteda,L.G.A.	Captain	-	Killed	9-17-14	
Armstrong, Dyer	Private	25th Inf.	Died	7-5-14	
Armstrong, Henry B.	Captain	13th Inf.	"	10-13-12	
Armstrong, John	Lieut.		Killed	8-15-14	
Arnold, Benedict	Private	25th Inf.	Died	--	
Arnold, Jesse	Private	13th Inf.	"	4-22-13	

Arnold, William	Private	Ky. Mil.	Died	2-10-15	
Ash, Joshua	"	Dragoons	"	--	
Ashby, George	"	16 Inf.	"	11-16-13	
Asher, Fred	"	Art.	"	April 1814	
Ashford, James	Seaman		Killed	10-30-12	
Ashford, James	"	Constitution	"	8-20-12	
Ashmead, William	Private	Art.	Died	10-13-14	
Ashton, Samuel	"	16 Inf.	"	11-15-13	
Ashton, Samuel	"	16 Inf.	"	11-11-13	
Askley, George C.	"	Ky. Mil.	"	10-19-12	
Asler, Jeremiah	"	2nd Art.	"	10-11-12	
Asquith	Midshipman	Comm.Flotilla	Killed	-	
Atkins, Thos. B.	Private	12th Inf.	Died	6-2-14	
Atkinson, John	Mate	Champ.Sqd.	Killed	9-11-14	
Atlee, Wm. Pitt	Colonel	1st Div.Pa.Mil.	Died	1815	
Atwood, Elisha	Private	11th Inf.	"	11-11-14	
Austin, Benjamin	"	14th Inf.	"	1-18-15	
Austin, Charles	"	9th Inf.	"	11-22-13	
Austin, Moses	Lieut.	2 Lt.Drag.	Killed	7-17-12	
Ausunt, Wm.	Private	14th Inf.	Died	1-10-15	
Avery, Elisha	"	25th Inf.	"	5-18-15	
Ayers, John	"	12th Inf.	"	5-2-14	
Ayers, John	"	--	"	8-15-13	Quebec Prison
Aymar, John H.	"	7th Inf.	"	5-23-14	
Axtell, Samuel	"	11th Inf.	"	11-28-12	

Babb, Benjamin	Sailor	New York	Died	1814	Dartmoor Prison
Babb, James	Private	3rd Art.	"	Nov.1812	
Babbit, F. H.	Lieut.	President	Killed	1-18-14	
Babcock, Caleb	Private	23rd Inf.	Died	7-25-14	
Bablista, John	Sailor	New York	"	11-21-14	Dartmoor Prison
Bacon, Edmund,	Private	Ky.Mil.	"	10-19-12	
Bacon, Francis	"	9th Inf.	"	11-18-13	
Bacon, Iabbec	"	9th Inf.	"	8-6-13	Quebec Prison
Backster, Charles	Seaman	Argus	Killed	8-14-13	
Backus,	Colonel	Sacketts Harbor	"	5-29-13	
Bactman, Ely	Sailor	Mass.	Died	1813	
Bagley, Benjamin	Private	23rd Inf.	"	1-8-15	
Bailey	Captain	1st Reg.Miss.Vols.	Killed	8-30-13	
Bailey, Israel	Sailor	Lawrence	"	8-10-13	
Bailey, John	Private	1st Rifles	Died	7-4-14	
Bailey, John	"	11th Inf.	"	4-6-13	
Bailey, Peter	"	25th Inf.	"	11-1-13	
Bailey, Moses	"	25th Inf.	"	--	

Name	Rank	Unit	Fate	Date	Place
Bailey, Moses	Private	Pa.	Died	2-17-15	Dartmoor Prison
Bailey, Thomas	Yeoman	Essex	Killed	3-28-14	
Bailey, Thomas	"	"	"	7-3-14	
Baker, Abijah	Sgt.	22nd Inf.	Died	5-14-13	
Baker, Amos	Private	21st Inf.	"	10-4-14	
Baker, Benjamin	"	12 Reg.N.Y.Mil.	"	2-14-13	Sacketts Harbor
Baker, Caleb	"	6th Inf.	"	Dec. 1813	
Baker, Claiborne	"	10th Inf.	"	11-30-14	
Baker, D.	"	Lt. Drag.	"	Oct. 1914	
Baker, Henry	"	26th Rangers	"	1-18-15	
Baker, Jacob	"	16th Inf.	"	3-23-13	
Baker, Joseph	"	7th U.S.Inf.	"	6-19-14	
Baker, Lewis	"	23rd Inf.	"	---	
Baker, Moses	"	11th Inf.	"	7-19-13	
Baker, Nathan	"	25th Inf.	"	7-20-13	
Baker, Stephen	"	25th Inf.	"	1-12-15	
Balbadge, Christopher	Sailor	Mass.	"	1-9-13	At Chatham
Baldwin, John		Mass.	"	12-5-13	Dartmoor Prison
Baldwin, Nathanial	Private	Dragoons	"	3-4-15	
Baldwinn, John		Mass.	"	12-5-14	Dartmoor Prison
Bale, Benjamin		N. H.	"	1-27-14	" "
Ball, Benjamin	Private	15th Inf.	"	6-6-14	
Ball, Cyrus	"	3rd Reg.N.J.Mil.	"	---	
Ball, David	"	22nd Inf.	"	12-9-13	
Ballard, Edward J.	Lieut.	Chesapeake	Killed	6-1-13	
Ballard, I.M.	Sgt.	21st Inf.	"	11-11-13	
Ballard, Linsey	Private	17th Inf.	Died	3-1-15	
Ballinger, Isaac	"	Ky. Mil.	"	10-7-13	
Bancroft, Nathanial	"	Art.	"	5-3-15	
Banett, Levi	"	15th Inf.	"	12-12-14	
Banham, William	"	12th Inf.	"	12-11-14	
Bank, Joseph	"	34th Inf.	"	10-8-14	
Bannett, Josa	Sailor	Pa. Buisy	"	1814	Dartmoor Prison
Banta, Abraham	Private	---	Killed	10-6-13	Battle of Thames
Barber, Henry		Va.	Died	12-25-14	Dartmoor Prison
Barber, James M.	Private	22nd Inf.	"	---	
Barber, John S.	"	135th Reg.Pa.Mil.	"	3-20-13	
Bard, Valentine	"	15th Inf.	"	12-24-12	
Barker, Charles		Va.	"	1-30-14	Dartmoor Prison
Barker, Peter		Mass.	"	11-28-14	" "
Barley, Peter	Private	25th Inf.	"	11-1-13	
Barnes, Elijah	Lt.Col.	N.Y.Mil.	"	Aug. 1815	
Barnes, Elijah	Private	23rd Inf.	"	8-20-14	
Barnham, John P.	"	13th Inf.	"	5-4-14	
Barnum, John P.	"	13th Inf.	"	4-20-14	
Barrel, Levi	"	16th Inf.	"	12-12-14	
Barren, Thomas	"	Va.	"	11-3-13	Dartmoor Prison
Barret, James		Pa.	"	12-8-13	" "
Barret, Jason		Pa.	"	12-8-14	" "
Barrett, Thomas	Private	25th Inf.	"	7-28-13	
Barron, Thomas		Va.	"	11-3-13	Dartmoor Prison
Barrows, David	Private	21st Inf.	"	4-1-15	
Barrows, John			"	12-13-12	
Barry,	Major	5th Reg.	"	---	
Bartlett, Reans			"	3-10-15	
Bartly, Wm.	Private		"	8-13-13	Quebec Prison
Barton, David	"	Tenn.Vol.Cav.Reg.	"	1815	
Barton, Samuel	Lieut.	---	"	11-9-13	

Name	Rank/Unit		Status	Date	Location
Bascom, Samuel	Private		Died	4-21-13	Quebec Prison
Basman, Adam	Private	12th Inf.	"	10-28-14	
Bass, Timothy	Private	9th Inf.	"	2-28-15	
Basta, Howel	Sailor	Mass.	"	1- 7-13	Chatham
Bates, Joseph	Private	4th Rifles	"		
Bates, Y. S.			"	11-18-14	Dartmoor Prison
Baton, Robert	Private	Ky. Mil.	"	1-19-15	
Bauchman, George	Private	22nd Inf.	"	11-27-13	
Baum, Whitfield	Private	Ky. Mil.	"	9-28-13	
Baxten, Alex	Private	1st Inf.		--	
Baxter, Andrew, Jr.	Lieut.	103rd Dist. Ga. Mil.	"	1814	
Bayless, Rees	Private	Tenn. Vols	"	10-29-14	
Baylet, Benjmn	Private	16th Inf.	"	7-7-13	
Bayley, Moses		Pa.	"	2-17-15	Dartmoor Prison
Beach, Samuel	Private	29th Inf.	"	--	
Beaden, George	Sailor	Essex	Killed	3-28-14	
Beadles, Harmon D.	Private	16th Inf.	Died	1813	
Beadly, Harman D.	Private	2nd Art.	"	10-14-12	
Beakly, Micheal	Private	15th Inf.	"	--	
Beals, Daniel	Private	11th Inf.	"	--	
Bean, Andrew	Private	33rd Inf.	"	--	
Bean, Jonah	Private	33rd Inf.	"	--	
Bean, William	Private	5th Reg..E. Tenn.Mil.	"	1815	
Bear, Adam	Private	19th Inf.	"	--	
Bear, John	Private	Ky. Mil.	"	12-22-14	
Beard, Philip	Private	U.S. Inf.	"	3- 4-14	
Beardsley, John	Private	13th Inf.	"	9-26-12	
Beasley, Major	1st Reg.Miss.Vols.		Killed	8-30-13	
Beaufort, Louis Capt.	Captain Mich. Mil.		Died	1814	
Beagley, Edward		35th Inf.	"	2-16-14	
Bebee, Aurora	Private	23rd Inf.	"	1- 2-14	
Beck, James		N.H.	"	1-14-14	Dartmoor Prison
Beckelshamer, Joseph	Private	14th Inf.	"	8-15-13	
Beedel, Timothy	Sargeant	2nd Drag.	"	12-19-12	
Beek, William		N.H.	"	1-19-15	Dartmoor Prison
Beeson, Thomas V.	Private	Art.	Killed	9-14-14	Fort McHenry
Belding, Jonathan	Private	11th Inf.	Died	6-25-13	
Bell, George	"	Ky. Mil.	"	9-13-13	
Bell, Isaiah	Captain	O.	"	1815	
Bell, James	Private	22nd Inf.	"	1-4-14	
Bell, John	Private	14th Rifles	"	1-14-13	
Bell, John	"	12th Inf.	"	4-7-14	
Bell, Jonathan	"	12th Inf.	"	--	
Bell, Joseph	"	16th Inf.	"	Feb. 1815	
Belinore, Peter	"	22nd Inf.	"	10-30-14	
Belknap, W.	Lieut.		Killed	9-17-14	
Belote, Abel	Private	13th Inf.	Died	9-14-14	
Benedict, Daniel	Private	25th Inf.	"	12-30-14	
Benham, William	Private	12th Inf.	"	12-11-14	
Benjamin		N.Y.	"	1-29-15	Dartmoor Prison
Benjamin, Jacob	Private	13th Inf.	"	3- 3-14	
Benjamin, Jesse	Private	3rd Rifles	"	11-28-13	

Name	Rank	Unit		Date	
Benn, William		Va.	Died	11-27-14	Dartmoor Prison
Bennet, Anthony	Private	4th Inv.	"	9-9-14	
Bennett, David	Seaman	Saratoga	Killed	9-11-14	
Bennett, John	Corp.	O. Mil	Died	1814	
Bennett, John	Private	30th Inf.	"	1-3-15	
Bennett, Lester	"	27th Inf.	"	--	
Bennett, Samuel	"		"	7-10-13	
Bennington, Thomas	"	29th Inf.	"	11-3-14	
Benson,	"	4th Inf.	"	12-2-14	
Benson, Nehemial	"	25th Inf.	"	10-10-13	
Bentley, Jonas	"	Art.	"	--	
Berkley, John	"	14th Inf.	"	5-30-15	
Berry, John	"	10th Inf.	"	--	
Berry, Peter		Baltimore	"	11-28-14	Dartmoor Prison
Berry, William	Private	33rd Inf.	"	10-10-13	
Betty, George		Maryland	"	2-14-15	Dartmoor Prison
Bevoit, John	Private	15th Inf.	"	11-21-14	
Bibb, James	"	20th Inf.	"	2-24-14	
Bidman, Peter	""	22nd Inf.	"	10-30-14	
Bigelow,	1 Lieut.	21st Inf.	Killed	11-11-13	
Bigelow, Aaron	1 "	21st Inf.	"	7-25-14	
Bigelow, Elnathan	Private	21st Inf.	Died	7-22-13	
Bigelow, John	"	Rifles	"	4-27-13	
Billings, Benjamin	"	9th Inf.	"	12-28-13	
Billings, Thomas	Sailor	N.Y.	"	Dec. 1813	
Bills, James S.		O. Mil.		--	
Bin, Peter		Va.	"	11-28-14	Dartmoor Prison
Bingham, Ralph	Private	11th Inf.	"	1-9-14	
Birc, James	"	4th Inf.	"	12-16-14	
Bird, John H.	Midshipman		Killed	10-30-12	
Bird, John H.	Sailor	President	"	9-11-14	
Birwell, William	Private	23rd Inf.	Died	10-31-14	
Bisbee, Noah	Sgt.	21st Inf.	"	--	
Bishop, Eleazer	Corp.	25th Inf.	"	--	
Bishop, James	Private	9th Inf.	"	11-11-13	
Bishop, John	"	41st Inf.	"	1-6-15	
Bishop, Richard	"	29th Inf.	"	9-6-14	
Bissell, John	"	11th Inf.	"	11-13-13	
Bissell, Moses	"	21st Inf.	"	2-12-15	
Blackburn, William	"	O. Mil.	"	1813	
Blackman, Moses	Sailor	Mass.	"	12-5-14	
Blackman, Simon		O. Mil.	"	--	
Blackwell, James	Private	10th Inf.	"	12-12-14	
Blagdell, Philip		N.H.	"	1-20-14	Dartmoor Prison
Blair, Asahel	Private	17th Inf.	"	11-13-14	
Blair, Richard	Seaman	Globe	Killed	11-1-13	
Blair, Thomas	Colonel	6th Co.Pa.Mil.	Died	1814	
Blaisdell, Ebenezer	Private	21st U.S.Inf.	"	4-12-13	
Blake, Beverly A.	"	17th U.S.Inf.	"	--	
Blake, Braxton	"	17th U.S.Inf.	"	1-22-13	
Blake, Dearborn	"	9th U.S.Inf.	"	11-19-13	
Blake, Henry	"	3rd Art.	"	Jan. 1814	

Name	Rank	Unit	Status	Date	Prison
Blake, Jon	Private		Died	2-23-13	Quebec Prison
Blakesley,	Ensign		Killed	9-17-14	
Blanchard, John	Private	5th Inf.	Died	8-30-14	
Blanchard, Nick			"	5-5-14	Dartmoor Prison
Blanchard, Nicholas			"	1815	Dartmoor Prison
Bland, Francis	Q.M.	Essex	Killed	7-3-14	
Bland, Francis	Q.M.	Essex	"	3-28-14	
Blaney, Daniel	2 Lieut.	3rd U.S. Art.	"	5-6-14	
Blasdill, Ebenezer		21st Inf.	Died	4-12-13	
Blasdill, Moses	Private	Lt. Art.	"	6-14-14	
Blasdill, William		N.H.	"	1-10-15	Dartmoor Prison
Blazed, Phillip		N.H.	"	1-10-13	Dartmoor Prison
Bledsoe, Jacob	Private	19th Inf.	"	10-15-14	
Bless, Reuben	"	25th Inf.	"	4-5-13	
Blew, John	Sailor	Frolic R.I.	"	1-1-13	Dartmoor Prison
Bliss, Timothy	Private	25th Inf.	"	10-20-13	
Blockburger, Fredk.	"	15th Inf.	"	--	
Blodget, Clark	"	N.Y. Vols.	"	9-13-14	
Bloomfield, Moses O.	2 Lieut.	15th Inf.	Killed	4-27-13	
Blossom, Elisha	Mate		"	11-11-13	
Blossom, Elisha	Mate	Enterprise	"	9-5-13	
Blythe, James E.	Private	Frenchtown	"	1-22-13	
Boardman, Richard	"	Lt. Art.	Died	1-9-14	
Boatman, John		Md.	"	11-23-13	Dartmoor Prison
Bocher, Henry	Private	14th N.Y. Vols.	"	8-23-14	
Boestler, Jacob	Captain		"	4-8-12	
Bogert, James J.	Private	13th Inf.	"	1-6-14	
Boggs, Francis	"	Pa. Dragoons	"	8-23-12	
Boise, Parnal		Champ. Squad.	Killed	9-11-14	
Bolden, John	Private	21st Inf.	Died	9-12-13	
Boley, Thomas	"	22nd Inf.	"	--	
Bolten, Royal	"	33rd Inf.	"	10-9-14	
Boner, William	"	4th Rifle	"	--	
Boon, Rhoderick	"	20th Inf.	"	1-29-15	
Boone, George	"	Ky. Mil.	"	8-20-13	
Booth, James	Sailor	Victory N.H.	"	1815	Dartmoor Prison
Booth, James		N.Y.	"	12-29-14	Dartmoor Prison
Boothe, Charles	Private	19th Inf.	"	8-31-13	
Boothe, Grey	"	10th Inf.	"	1-25-15	
Boothe, Nathaniel	"	20th Rifles	"	Dec. 1812	
Boran, John	"	5th Inf.	"	--	
Boughton, Seymour	Lt. Col.	12th Cav.,N.Y.	Killed	12-30-13	
Boulder, Mortimer, Jr.	Private	14th Rifles	Died	10-19-14	
Bourge, Daniel		N.H.	"	1-17-15	Dartmoor Prison
Boutelle, David		Mass. Mil.	"	8-5-16	
Boynton, Samuel	Private	Art.	"	9-7-14	
Bow, Stephen	"		"	8-27-13	Quebec Prison
Bowan, Benjamin	"	38th Inf.	"	June 1814	
Bowen, Amos	"	9th Inv.	"	8-21-14	
Bowen, Thomas	"	O	"	1815	
Bowen, Thomas	"	14th Inf.	"	2-7-15	
Bowers, Benjmn	"	25th	"	11-14-13	
Bowler, William	"	Ky. Inf.	"	10-31-14	

Name	Rank	Unit	Fate	Date	Notes
Bowers, Milton	Sgt.	13th Inf.	Died	--	
Bowles, Henry	Private	15th Inf.	"	7-20-13	
Bowman, Adam	"	12th Inf.	"	10-28-14	
Bowman, Fran	"	45th Inf.	"	3-6-15	
Bowman, Gilbert	"	26th Inf.	"	11-8-13	
Bowman, John	"	U.S. Inf.	"	4-16-14	
Bowman, John	"	12th Inf.	"	10-28-14	
Bowser,	"	Pa. Mil..	"	- 1813	
Boyd, Thomas	"	34th Inf.	"	11-11-13	
Bozman, Daniel	"	--	"	4-21-13	
Brace, Stephen	"	25th Inf.	"	1-7-15	
Bracel, Stephen	"	25th Inf.	"	11-7-14	
Braden, George	"	12th Reg.	"	.5-21-14	
Bradfield, Joseph	"	2nd Dragoons	"	11-11-13	
Bradfield, Samuel	"	4th Rifles	"	11-2-14	
Bradford, Hamilton	Captain	Tenn.	Killed	1-24-14	
Bradford, James	Prviate	3rd Inf.	Died	2-28-14	
Bradford, Lemuel	Captain	21st Inf.	Killed	9-17-14	
Bradford, Larkin	Lieut.	Tenn.	"	11-9-13	
Bradford, Timothy	Private	11th Inf.	Died	4-14-14	
Bradley, George	"	13th Inf.	"	8-18-13	
Bradley, James	"	16th Rifles	"	12-22-12	
Bradlow, And.	"	13th Inf.	"	11-11-13	
Bradt, Samuel A.	"	3rd Art.	"	8-1-13	
Brady, George	"	27th Inf.	"	10-13-14	
Brady, Robert	"	16th Inf.	"	5-27-13	
Brady, William		N.Y.	"	3-29-15	Dartmoor Prison
Brady, William		N.H.	"	1-20-15	Dartmoor Prison
Brailsford, Joseph	Midshipman	Alligator		7-1-14	
Bramot, Dan	Private	25th Inf.	"	10-31-14	
Bramin, Benjamin	"	16th Inf.	"	5-27-13	
Branch, Elijah	"	21st Inf.	"	7-25-14	
Brandon, Alexander	Colonel	104th Reg.W.Va.Mil.	"	3-13-13	
Brasier, Daniel B.	Private	6th Inf.	"	Dec. 1813	
Bray, Hezekiah		Mass.	"	11-20-13	Dartmoor Prison
Bray, Ezikiah		Mass.	"	11-20-14	Dartmoor Prison
Brazur, Thomas	Private	14th Inf.	"	6-10-15	
Breevort, John	"	15th Inf.	"	--	
Bremesholtz, Henry	"	Art.	"	11-26-14	
Brewer, Zachariah	"	14th Inf.	"	--	
Briant, Jeremiah S.	"	45th Inf.	"	1-3-15	
Brice, James	"	Art.	"	12-16-14	
Brice, Robert	Seaman		Killed	10-30-12	
Brice, Robert	"	Constitution	"	8-20-12	
Brickell, William	"	Saratoga-Lake Champ	"	9-11-14	
Bridges, Daniel	Private	4th Inf.	Died	11-18-14	
Bridges, Joseph	"	Art.	"	--	
Bridges, William	"	Ky. Mil.	"	1-20-15	
Bridges, William	"	" "	"	11-13-13	
Briggs, John	"	33rd Inf.	"	10-3-13	
Brill, Robert	Corp.	Art.	"	10-14-12	
Brill, William	Private	12th Inf.	"	1-21-14	

Brink, John	Private	Dragoons	Died	1813	
Bristow, Barney	"	6th Ky. Mil.	"	12-24-12	
Britton, Boykin	"	10th Inf.	"	9-27-14	
Britton, Nathaniel	"	1st Inf.	"	1-3-15	
Brock, George	"	7th Inf.	"	4-29-14	
Brooks, Eli	"	10th Inf.	"	1-30-15	
Brooks, Herman	"	25th Inf.	"	11-14-13	
Brooks, John	"	4th Rifles	"	5-31-15	
Brooks, John	Lieut.	Marine Lawrence	"	12-31-13	
Brooks, John	"	Lawrence	Killed	9-10-13	
Brooks, John	Private	2nd Art.	Died	--	
Brooks, Samuel	Lieut.		Killed	12-23-14	
Brooks, William J.	Corp.	15th Inf.	Died	--	
Brooks, William	Private	15th Inf.	"	3-3-14	
Broom, James	1 Lieut.	Chesapeake	Killed	6-1-13	
Bross, Garrett	Private	76th Inf.	Died	--	
Brown, Aaron	"	Dragoons	"	11-9-13	
Brown, Alex	"	14th N.Y. Vols.	"	9-16-14	
Brown, Charles		Md.	"	2-17-15	Dartmoor Prison
Brown, Connel	"	5th Inf.	"	10-19-14	
Brown, Edward	Sailor	Mass.	"	5-3-13	
Brown, Frederick	Private	16th Inf.	"	3-12-13	
Brown, George		N.Y.	"	2-11-15	Dartmoor Prison
Brown, Henry	Private	17th Inf.	"	--	
Brown, Hiram	"	1st Rifles	"	Dec. 1813	
Brown, Jacob	"	Inf. E. Tenn.	"	1814	
Brown, James	Seaman	Lawrence	Killed	12-31-13	
Brown, Jesse	"	Maine	Died	6-11-13	Chatham
Brown, John Sr.	Private	Art.	"	3-5-13	
Brown, John	Seaman		Killed	10-30-12	
Brown, John	Seaman	Constitution	"	8-20-12	
Brown, John	Private	17th Inf.	Died	1-11-15	
Brown, John Riggs	2 Lieut.	3rd Cav.Md.Mil.	"	10-3-14	
Brown, Joshua	Seaman	Globe	Killed	11-1-13	
Brown, Parker	Private	45th Inf.	Died	8-28-14	
Brown, Peter	"	7th Inf.	"	4-5-14	
Brown, Thomas	Seaman	N.Y. Macedonian	Killed	10-30-12	
Brown, Thomas	Private	22nd Inf.	Died	5-2-14	
Brown, Thomas	Lieut.		Killed	9-17-14	
Brown, Walter	Private	25th Inf.	Died	1-4-15	
Brown, William	"	0	"	1813	
Brown, William	"	38th Inf.	"	2-21-14	
Browne, Robert	Seaman	Essex	Killed	3-18-14	
Browne, Thomas	Sailor	Essex	"	3-28-14	
Browning, Almond	Sgt.	6th Ky. Mil.	Died	12-6-12	
Brumesholtz, Henry	Private	3rd Art.	"	--	
Brumley, Amos	25th Inf.		"	4-25-13	
Bruce, Jeremiah	Private	4th Inf.	"	12-12-14	
Brush, Ely	"	41st Inf.	"	12-4-14	
Brush, John R.	"	2nd Art.	"	12-26-12	
Brush, W. S.	Lieut.	Capture Guerrier	Killed	--	
Bryant, Ephraim	Private	10th Inf.	Died	10-24-12	

Name	Rank	Unit	Status	Date	Location
Bryant, Hezekiah	Private	13th Inf.	Died	4-30-14	
Bryant, John	"	15th Inf.	"	11-21-14	
Bryant, Louis		N.C.	"	11-3-14	Dartmoor Prison
Bryant, Platt	"	41st Inf.	"	2-1-15	
Bryen, Lewis		S.C.	"	11-5-14	Dartmoor Prison
Bryson, John		Va.	"	1-23-14	Dartmoor Prison
Buchanan, Samuel	Private	15th Inf.	"	Aug. 1813	
Buchanon, Joseph	"	5th Inf.	"	11-24-12	
Buckingham, Jonas	"	41st Inf.	"	2-26-13	
Buckingham, Jonas	"	N.Y. Mil.	"	1815	
Buckley, John	"	12th Rifles	"	4-1-13	
Buckman, Francis	"	1st Art.	"	2-2-14	
Buel,	Captain		Killed	9-17-14	
Buel, Alec. M.	Private	16th Rifles	Died	8-1-13	
Bugbee, Stephen D	"	3rd Art.	"	3-20-13	
Buker, William	"	2nd Art.	"	8-15-14	
Bull, Benj. S.	Sgt.		"	10-20-13	Quebec Prison
Bull, Thomas	Private	O	"	1815	
Bullard, Thomas	"	42nd Rifles	"	10-16-14	
Bundy, Gurdon	"	25th Inf.	"	11-30-13	
Bunker, Nicholas	Sailor	Mass.	"	6-5-13	Chatham
Bunker, Alexander	Private	N.Y. Mil.	"	Mar. 1813	
Bunnel, Isaac	"	42nd Inf.	"	12-24-14	
Burbage, Henry		Va.	"	12-25-14	Dartmoor Prison
Burch, John	Private	Lt. Drag.	"	9-25-14	
Burch, Peter		Pa.	"	3-13-15	
Burch, Theophilus	Private	14th Inf.	"	--	
Burchsted, H. A.	Lieut.	2nd Inf.	Killed	11-30-13	
Billings, Burdick	Champ. Squad		"	9-11-14	
Burford, William	Sgt.	20th Inf.	Died	8-2-13	
Burghardt, Adolphus	2 Lt.		Killed	7-25-14	
Burghardt,	2 Lt	9th Inf.	"	11-11-13	
Burhams, Simon	Private	Lt. Art.	Died	--	
Burkaus, Simon	"	1st Art.	"	3-24-14	
Burland, John	"		"	4-20-13	Quebec Prison
Burley, Henry		N.Y.	"	12-2-14	Quebec Prison
Burley, Henry		N.Y.	"	12-2-13	Quebec Prison
Burnet, Samuel	Private	15th Inf.	"	--	
Burnet, William	Drummer	135th Reg. Pa.Mil.	"	3-2-15	
Burnham, Abraham		Mass.	"	3-25-15	Ashburton
Burnham, Daniel	Q.M.	Chesapeake	Killed	6-1-13	
Burnham, Joseph	Sgt.		Died	8-15-14	
Burns, John	Private	14th Inf.	"	--	
Burrans, Semor	Private	1st Art.	"	3-24-14	
Burrell, William	"	23rd Inf.	"	10-31-14	
Burrill, Benjamin	Seaman	Saratoga	Killed	9-11-14	
Burrough, Thomas	Private	Ky. Mil.	Died	5-5-13	
Burrows,	Lieut.		Killed	11-11-13	
Burrows, William	Lt. Com.	Enterprise	"	9-5-13	
Burt, Jacob	Private		Died	July 1814	
Busby, James	"	41st Inf.	"	1-30-15	
Bush, Abrah	"		"	3-22-13	Quebec Prison

Bush, Edward	Private	Ky. Inf.	Died	10-31-14	
Bush, William S.	1 Lt.	Marines-Constitution	Killed	8-20-12	
Buswell, Reuben A.	Private	11 Inf.	Died	1-3-13	
Butler, David	"	7th Inf.Conn.Mil.	"	3-3-15	
Butler, Henry	Mag. Gen.1st Div.N.H.Mil.		"	7-20-13	
Butler, Israel	Private	16th Inf.	"	12-17-12	
Butler, James	Sailor	Boston	"	12-5-14	Chatham
Butler, John		Del.	"	2-22-15	Dartmoor Prison
Butler, Joshua	Private	7th U.S. Inf.	"	4-17-14	
Butler, Thomas	Q.M.	Saratoga	Killed	9-11-14	
Butler, Thomas	Private	17th Inf.	Died	12-21-14	
Butler, Thomas	Seaman	Lawrence	Killed	12-31-13	
Butler, William	Private	25th Inf.	Died	11-8-13	
Butler, William	"	Frenchtown	Killed	1-22-13	
Butler, William	"	21st Inf.	Died	2-21-14	
Butler, William	Sailor	Baltimore	"	2-28-14	Chatham
Butman, John			"	11-23-14	Dartmoor Prison
Butt, Gan	Private	10th Rifles	"	5-10-13	
Butts, Samuel	Captain	Ga. Mil.	Killed	1-27-14	
Butter, John		Del.	Died	2-23-15	Dartmoor Prison
Byard, Peter	Private	39th Regt.	Killed	9-14-14	
Byard, John C.	"	U.S. Vols.	"	9-14-14	
Byron, Edward	"	22nd Inf.	Died	9-13-14	
Byron, Edward	"	22nd Inf.	"	8-25-14	

Cadell, William	Corp.	Art.	Died	Dec. 1814	
Cady, Jonas	Private	25th Inf.	"	11-2-12	
Cady, Aden	"	11th Inf.	"	8-9-14	
Cain, Henry	"	12th Inf.	"	7-18-13	
Cain, John	"	45th Inf.	"	9-21-14	
Caldwell, Andrew	"	22nd Inf.	"	10-30-14	
Callaway, James	"		Killed	3-7-15	
Calvin, William	"	Art. Reg.	Died	11-3-14	
Cambell, George	Sailor	.	Killed	4-6-15	Dartmoor Prison
Camp, William	Private	8th Inf.	Died	11-15-14	
Campbell, Archld	"	10th Inf.	Killed	12-10-13	
Campbell, Charles	"	30th Inf.	"	10-3-14	
Campbell, Frank	"	16th Inf.	"	11-11-13	
Campbell, George K.	"	7th Inf.	Died	12-3-14	
Campbell, Henry	Sailor	Pa.	"	3-22-15	Dartmoor Prison
Campbell, James	"	N.Y.	"	4-5-15	Dartmoor Prison

Campbell, John	Private	20th Inf.	Died	2-19-14	
Campbell, John	"	42nd Inf.	"	4-21-15	
Campbell, Robert	" Ohio	wounded in battle	"	1-21-13	
Canpeach, Samuel		N.Y.	"	1-17-13	Dartmoor Prison
Canpeachy, C.		Carthyogiua	"	1-19-14	Dartmoor Prison
Cammeron, John	Private	16th Inf.	·"	7-13-13	
Cane, John	"	45th Inf.	"	9-21-14	
Canelle, Castle	"	17th Inf.	"	12-21-14	
Canfield, Gold	"	61st Reg.N.Y.Mil.	"	Dec.1814	
Cannady, Micah	"	23rd Inf.	"	1-20-13	
Cannon, James	"	6th Inf.	"	Oct.1812	
Cannon, James	"	16th Inf.	"	Aug.1814	
Cannon, John	"	17th Inf.	"	8-15-14	
Cannon, Martin	"	22nd Inf.	"	9-10-14	
Capill, Samuel	"	17th Inf.	"	12-9-14	
Capiner, Daniel F.	Sailor	Essex	Killed	3-28-14	
Capland, Thomas	"	S.C.	Died	5-4-13	
Capps, Joshua	Private	Ky.Mil.	"	12-28-14	
Carlin, William	"	Coast Art.	"	1-1-15	
Carlisle, Henry	"	6th Ky.Mil.	"	12-2-12	
Carlisle, James	Sailor	Saratoga	Killed	9-11-14	
Carlisle, James	Private	15th Inf.	Died	9-11-14	
Carlton, Robert	"	Va. Mil.	"	12-1-14	
Carlton, Robert	2 cps.	Va.Mil	"	12-27-14	
Carmer, Nicholas, N.	Private	46th Inf.	"	3-24-15	
Carnacomb, George	"	5th Inf.	"	12-22-14	
Carney, John	Sailor	Va.	"	10-16-13	Dartmoor Prison
Carpenter,Abraham	Private	6th Co.3 Bat.L.C.M.D.	"	1815	
Carpenter, Ephraim	"	24th Inf.	"	Mar. 1814	
Carpenter, John	"	Ky. Mil.	"	9-28-13	
Carpenter, Samuel	"	11th Inf.	"	--	
Carr, Candy	"	13th Inf.	"	10-20-12	
Carr, D.	"	13th Inf.	"	1814	
Carr, James	"	20th Inf.	"	--	
Carr, Isaiah	"	5th Inf.	"	10-19-14	
Carroll, Philip	"	2nd Art.	"	12-10-13	
Carroll, St. Clair	"	Art.	"	--	
Carson, John	"	N.C. Mil.	"	3-7-15	
Carter, Andrew	"	30th Inf.	"	8-16-14	
Carter, Deal	"	N.Y.	"	10-3-13	Dartmoor Prison
Carter, George W.	"	Ky.Mil.Vols	"	10-5-13	
Carter, John	Sailor	Chesapeake	Killed	6-1-13	
Carter, Roger	"	Lake Champ	"	9-6-14	
Carter, Rogers	Master	Preble	"	9-11-14	
Carter, Rogers		Lake Champ	"	9-11-14	
Carter, Thomas	Sailor	Va.	Died	11-23-13	Chatham
Carter, William	Private	Drag.	"	--	
Carter, William	"	N.Y.	"	5-5-14	Dartmoor Prison
Carter, William	"	N.Y.Zephyr	"	1814	" "
Carty, James	Mate	Lawrence	Killed	12-31-13	
Carver, William	Private	--	Died	9-12-13	
Case, Henry	"	1st Inf.	"	1-11-15	
Casey, Hugh	"	25th Inf.	"	6-27-13	
Casey, Nathaniel	"	2nd Art.	"	Nov. 1813	

Cash, Isaac	Ensign	Pa. Mil.	Died	4-12-13	
Cash, Peter	Sgt.	Ky. Mil.	"	1-8-15	
Cassaday, M.	Private	38th Inf.	"	3-26-14	
Cassell, John	"	Ky. Mil. Inf.	"	3-30-15	
Cassidey, John	"	Pa. Vols.	"	9-25-14	
Casson, William	"	20th Inf.	"	2-2-14	
Castle, Canello	"	17th Inf.	"	12-21-14	
Caswell, Lemuel	"	3rd Art.	"	9-6-13	
Cater, Timothy	"	2nd Art.	"	9-18-13	
Cealing, John	"	17th Inf.	"	1-13-14	
Cempler, Wm. H.	Major		Killed	10-12-12	
Chace, David	Private	13th Inf.	Died	Oct. 1812	
Chadwich, Benjamin	"	9th Inf.	"	--	
Chadwich, Elias	"	25th Inf.	"	1-16-15	
Chamberlain, Sam	"	Art.	"	--	
Chambers, Peter	"	6th Inf.	"	2-3-14	
Chambliss	Ensign	1st Reg.Miss.Vols.	Killed	8-30-13	
Champlin, George G.	Private	25th Inf.	Died	8-21-14	
Champlin, George	"	25th Inf.	"	9-30-14	
Chapman, William	"	O	"	1813	
Chariton, James	"	22nd Inf.	"	7-25-14	
Chandler, Charles	"	9th Inf.	"	7-27-13	
Chandler, James	"	3rd Reg. Ga.Mil.	"	1815	
Chandler, Joshua S.	"	3rd Art.	"	2-19-14	
Chandler, Ray	"	23rd Inf.	"	9-23-13	
Chandler, Simeon	Sailor	Mass.	"	10-25-13	Dartmoor Prison
Chandler, Thomas	Corp.	21st Inf.	"	3-22-15	
Chase, Benjamin	Private	4th Inf.	"	2-11-15	
Chase, Charles	"	25th Inf.	"	7-26-13	
Chase, George W.	"	45th Inf.	"	11-9-14	
Chase, John	"	9th Inf.	"	11-11-13	
Chase, Nathan	"	9th Inf.	"	11-29-13	
Chase, Richard	"	25th Inf.	"	9-16-13	
Chase, Simon	"	34th Inf.	"	8-15-14	
Chase, William	"	26th Inf.	"	12-5-13	
China, Francis	Lieut.		Killed	1-22-13	
Cheever, John	Seaman	Constitution	"	--	
Cheeves, John	"	Constitution	"	12-29-12	
Chester, Bingham	Private	9th Inf.	Died	11-11-13	
Chitesten, Abner	"	15th Inf.	"	12-4-14	
Choate, John	"	45th Inf.	"	10-1-14	
Christopher, John(Jungkwith"		Pa. Mil.	"	11-23-14	
Christie, Alex	"	15th Inf.	"	Oct. 1813	
Christie, John	"	13th Inf.	"	5-25-14	
Christy,	Sailor	Baltimore	"	5-25-13	Chatham
Christy, John	Private	22nd Inf.	"	12-7-12	
Church, Benj.	"	21st Inf.	"	Sept. 1813	
Church, Moses	"	11th Inf.	"	3-2-13	
Church, William	Ensign	O	"	1813	
Churchill, Oliver	Private		"	7-28-13	Quebec Prison
Chushman, Daniels	"	11 Inf.	"	12-25-13	
Cinkhorn, John	"	Ky. Mil.	"	12-2-14	
Civites, Alvin	"	25th Inf.	"	1813	

Name	Rank	Unit	Fate	Date	Place
Clagett, Levi	Lieut.	Balto.Fencibles	Killed	9-14-14	Fort McHenry
Clapham, Stephen	Private	34th Inf.	Died	8-30-14	
Claridge, William	"	21st Inf.	"	1-3-14	
Clark, Abial	"	25th Inf.	"	8-1-13	
Clark, Charles	"	14th Inf.	"	10-7-14	
Clark, David	"	2nd Art.	"	7-31-13	
Clark, George	"	Ky. Mil.	"	5-5-13	
Clark, Israel	Seaman	Madison	Killed	4-24-13	
Clark, John	Private	2nd Art.	Died	5-27-13	
Clark, John	Midshipman	Scorpion	Killed	12-31-13	
Clark, Jonathan	Private	9th Inf.	Died	11-11-13	
Clark, Jonathan	"		"	11-16-13	Quebec Prison
Clark, Joseph	"	Art.	"	4-19-15	
Clark, Joseph	Captain		Killed	5-5-13	Dudley's Defeat
Clark, Joseph	Private	Ky. Mil	Died	5-5-13	
Clark, Joshua	"	2nd Art.	"	12-5-13	
Clark, Philip	"	9th Inf.	"	11-28-13	
Clark, Randolph	"	20th Inf.	"	1-21-15	
Clark, Samuel	"	9th Inf.	"	3-8-15	
Clark, Shedrick	"	25th Inf.	"	11-1-14	
Clark, Simon		New Eng.	"	1-24-14	Dartmoor Prison
Clark, Simon	Private	11th Inf.	"	7-3-13	
Clark, Simon		N.E. Snap Dragon	"	1913	Dartmoor Prison
Clark, Thomas F	Private	7th Inf.	"	--	
Clark, Thomas	"	22nd Inf.	"	10-17-14	
Clark, Waters	Major	13th Inf.	"	6-28-14	
Clark, William		R.I.	"	10-20-13	Dartmoor Prison
Clark, William Joseph		Ky. Mil.	"	5-5-13	
Clarke, Benjamin	Private	21st Inf.	"	--	
Clarke, Charles	"	14th Inf.	"	10-7-14	
Clarke, John	Sailor	Scorpion	Killed	9-10-13	
Clarke, Joseph	Private	18th Inf.	Died	3-20-14	
Clarke, Stephen	Captain	N.Y.	Killed	10-13-12	
Clarke, William	Private		Died	9-5-13	Quebec Prison
Clarke, William		Va.	"	7-4-14	Dartmoor Prison
Clarke, William		N. Eng.	"	7-10-13	Dartmoor Prison
Clauson, Peter		U.S. Inf.	"	12-26-14	
Claxton, Jeremiah	Private	Ky. Mil.	"	2-10-15	
Clemens, Henry	"	25th Inf.	"	11-15-13	
Clement, David	Sgt.		"	--	Quebec Prison
Clement, Joseph	Private	42nd Inf.	"	6-6-15	
Clemm, John	Sgt.	Balto.Fencibles	Killed	9-14-14	Fort McHenry
Clemons, James	Private	7th Inf.	Died	4-28-14	
Clifflaw, Thomas	"	18th Inf.	"	8-9-14	
Clifford, Lares	"	Art.	"	8-11-14	
Clintick,	"	19th Inf.	"	9-13-14	
Clinton, John	Sailor	Essex	Killed	3-28-14	
Closson, William	Private	16th Inf.	Died	1-29-13	
Clough, Isaac	Sailor	Mass	"	4-16-13	Chatham
Coal, John		Md.	"	11-26-14	Dartmoor Prison
Cobb, Philo	Private	11th Inf.	"	2-22-13	
Cobb, Stephen	"	25th Inf.	"	11-18-13	
Cobbey, A.	"	18th Inf.	"	9-18-14	
Coburn, Charles	"	9th Inf.	"	6-1-13	

Coburn, Jonathan	Private	25th Inf.	Died	--	
Coburn, Pelatiah	"	21st Inf.	"	12-10-13	
Coburn, Reuben	"	Art.	"	12-17-13	
Cochran, William R.	"	13th Inf.	"	10-13-12	
Cochran, William	Sgt.	O.	"	1814	
Cockrill, Thomas	1 Lieut.	3rd Art.Brig.Md.Mil.	"	10-1-15	
Coff, John		L.I.	"	1814	Dartmoor Prison
Coffee, John		L.I.	"	12-4-14	Dartmoor Prison
Coffee, Joseph	Private	25th Inf.	"	9-27-14	
Cogswell, Allanson	"		"	3-5-13	Quebec Prison
Colby, Nicholas	"	4th Inf.	"	2-24-15	
Cole, Ezra	"	26th Inf.	"	3-3-15	
Cole, James	"	Wiscasset	"	4-20-13	Dartmoor Prison
Cole, John		Balto.	"	11-26-13	Dartmoor Prison
Cole, John		N.H. Mil.	"	1814	In Service
Cole, John	Private	16th Inf.	"	11-27-14	
Coleman, John	Seaman	Saratoga	Killed	9-11-14	
Coleman, Noah	Private	3rd Inf.	Died	--	
Coleman, William		N.C.	"	11-5-14	Dartmoor Prison
Colgan, John	"	16th Inf.	"	5-26-14	
Colier, James	"	10th Inf.	"	5-30-14	
Collins, John	"	29th Inf.	"	10-9-14	
Collins, John	"	11th Inf.	"	7-5-13	
Collins, John		Phila.	"	10-7-13	Dartmoor Prison
Collins, John	Private	5th Inf.	"	12-30-14	
Collins, John	"	11th Inf.	"	3-23-13	
Collins, John	"	25th Inf.	"	6-14-13	
Collins, Jno.		Md.	"	8-7-13	Dartmoor Prison
Colly, John	Private	21st Inf.	"	12-29-13	
Colver, John	"	Ohio	"	1814	
Combe, Isaac	"		"	12-22-13	Quebec Prison
Combs, James		Me	"	3-5-13	Dartmoor Prison
Comegys, John	"	32nd Inf.	"	10-31-13	
Comstock, Elihu	"	25th Inf.	"	3-1-15	
Condit, Cyrus Ball	"	3rd Reg.N.J.Mil.	"	1814	
Coney, Edward	"	20th Inf.	"	1813	
Congar, Moses	"	15th Inf.	"	2-8-15	
Congdon, Elisha	1 Lieut.	Drag.	"	5-31-13	
Congdon, James		Mass.	"	11-11-13	Dartmoor Prison
Conger, Abraham Benj.	Capt.	Ga.Mil.22nd Reg.	"	1814	
Congleton, David	Private	9th Inf.	"	11-11-13	
Conker, Michael	"	1st Inf.	"	8-23-14	
Conklin, John	"	23rd Inf.	"	8-17-13	
Conklin, Lewis H.	"	46th Inf.	"	1-6-15	
Conlon, James	"	5th Inf.	"	12-12-14	
Connell, Danl.	"	23rd Inf.	"	12-6-14	
Conner, Isaac	"	7th Inf.	"	5-14-14	
Conner, John	"		"	4-6-15	Dartmoor Prison
Conner, Patrick	Seaman	Constitution	Killed	12-29-12	
Conner, William	Private	32nd Inf.	Died	6-28-13	
Connor, James	"	14th Inf.	"	May 1813	
Conrad, Peter	"	22nd Inf.	"	4-19-19	
Constant, Jacob	"	Ky. Mil.	"	11-20-13	
Convess, James	"	3rd Art.	"	9-18-14	

Cook, Abraham	Private	Art.	Died	6-30-12	
Cook, Benj.	"	Md.	"	4-6-13	Dartmoor Prison
Cook, Calwell	"	29th Inf.	"	6-25-14	
Cook, James	"	11th Drg.	"	--	
Cook, Nathaniel	"	11th Inf.	"	4-25-13	
Cook, William	"	14th Inf.	"	4-21-14	
Coon, Henry	"	23rd Inf.	"	3-13-15	
Coons, John	"	25th Inf.	"	11-7-13	
Cooper, Enoch	"	26th Inf.	"	11-13-13	
Cooper, George	Cpt.	7th Inf.	"	3-20-14	
Cooper, Peter	Private	23rd Inf.	"	4-10-15	
Cooper, Sarshel	Captain	Com.Mo.Fort	Killed	4-6-15	
Cooper, Thomas	Private	14th N.Y. Vols	Died	8-14-14	
Cooper, Thos.		R.I.	"	11-8-14	Dartmoor Prison
Cooper, Thomas		N.C.	"	11-8-13	Dartmoor Prison
Cooper, William	Seaman	Constitution	Killed	12-29-12	
Core, Thomas	Private	15th Inf.	Died	3-4-14	
Cornelius, John	"	38th Inf.	"	--	
Corning, David	"	25th Inf.	"	8-31-14	
Cornish, Charles		Md.	"	1-16-13	Dartmoor Prison
Corry, Asa	Private		"	10-20-13	Quebec Prison
Cory, Abraham	"	26th Inf.	"	10-21-13	
Cosby, Garland	"	8th Inf.	"	11-3-14	
Cotman, Joseph	"	16th Inf.	"	6-15-14	
Cottars, Joseph	"	25th Inf.	"	2-15-15	
Cottemore, Peleg	"	9th Inf.	"	12-18-13	
Cotten, Seth	"		"	9-2-13	Quebec Prison
Cotten, William	"	9th Inf.	"	11-18-13	
Couch, Joseph	Landsman	Saratoga	Killed	9-11-14	
Courrier, James	Private	11th Inf.	Died	2-5-13	
Courter, James	"	23rd Inf.	"	--	
Covington, Leonard	Brig.Gen.		"	11-14-13	of wounds
Cowell, John G.	Lieut.	Essex	Killed	3-28-14	
Cox, Joseph	Private	16th Inf.	Died	7-5-13	
Cox, R. L. B.	"	18th Inf.	"	10-13-14	
Coyle, William	"	22nd Inf.	"	--	
Craft, Gilbert	"	Ky. Mil.	"	2-17-15	
Craft, Samuel	"	25th Inf.	"	Feb. 1815	
Craig, John	"	15th Inf.	"	8-24-13	
Craig, Peter	Captain	Rangers	Killed	5-24-15	
Crannell, Cornelius	Private	16th Inf.	Died	11-11-13	
Cranston, James	"	25th Inf.	"	6-6-13	
Cranston, William	Seaman	Lawrence	Killed	12-31-13	
Crawford, Absalom	Private	13th Inf.	Died	--	
Crawford, Robert	"	4th Inf.	"	4-2-13	
Creighton, Samuel		9th Inf.	"	1-23-14	
Cremer, David	Private	14th Inf.	"	12-1-12	
Crenshaw, Charles	"	74th Reg.Va.Mil.	"	1814	
Crist, Philip	Sailor	Wasp	Killed	10-18-12	
Critishlow, John	Private	1st Inf.	Died	8-19-14	
Crittenden, Jared	"	2nd Art.	"	May 1814	
Crittenton, Jason	Corp.	55th Inf. N.Y.Mil.	"	3-17-13	
Crooker, Calvin	Private	9th Inf.	"	10-16-14	
Crosby, Benjamin	Sgt.	23rd Inf.	"	10-27-12	

Crosby, Joseph	Seaman	Alligator	Died	7-1-14	
Croshaw, William	Private	6th Inf.	"	Feb. 1813	
Cross, William	Sgt.	4th Inf.	"	12-13-14	
Crossman, Seth	Private	2nd Inf.	"	7-25-14	
Crouch,	Captain	N.Y. Vols.	"	4-25-15	
Crouch, Isaac	Private	Ky. Mil.	"	1-8-15	
Crouse, John	"	22nd Inf.	"	9-15-14	
Crow, John	"	23rd Inf.	"	7-13-13	
Crow, Thomas	"	Frenchtown	Killed	1-22-13	
Crowley, Asa	"	7th Inf.	Died	4-3-14	
Crum, William	"	Ky. Mil.	"	10-22-13	
Crutchlow, John	"	1st Inf.	"	8-19-14	
Cryer, William	"	8th Inf.	"	8-5-14	
Cummings, Eleazer	"	21st Inf.	"	10-9-13	
Cummins, James	"	22nd Inf.	"	9-11-14	
Cummins, John	"	11th Inf.	"	12-15-12	
Cummins, Thomas	Sailor	Wasp	Killed	10-18-12	
Cunningham, Andrew	Private	24th Inf.	Died	4-23-15	
Cunningham, John	"	3rd Rifles	"	Mar. 1815	
Cunningham, M	"	41st Inf.	"	1-17-15	
Cunningham, Robert	"	19th Inf.	"	5-16-13	
Cunningham, William	"	17th Inf.	"	3-25-14	
Currier, Jonathan	"	21st Inf.	"	8-11-13	
Curry, Archibald	"	11th Inf.	"	4-5-13	
Curry, Robert	"	16th Inf.	"	8-7-13	
Curry, Thomas	"	Drag.	"	--	
Curser, William	"	11th Inf.	"	1812	
Curthburth, Joseph	"	1st Art.	"	2-16-14	
Curtis, D. B.	"	3rd Art.	"	11-30-12	
Cushing, Daniel Lewis	Brig.Gen.	O. Mill	Drowned	3-29-15	
Cushing, Reginelich	Private	21st Inf.	Died	June 1813	
Custer, Jacob		Art.	"	Sept. 1814	
Cutter, John		9th Inf.	"	12-20-13	
Cutter, Jonas	Private	11th Inf.	"	2-2-13	
Cuyler, William Howe	Major		Killed	10-9-12	At Black Rock
Cuyler,	Major	U.S.Gunboat	"	Jan. 1815	New Orleans

Dager, Joseph	Private	4th Inf.	Died	2-21-14	
Dagget, Thomas		Mass.	"	3-14-14	Dartmoor Prison
Dalrymple, Henry	Private	Art.	"	--	
Dalton, William		Ga.	"	5-10-14	Dartmoor Prison

Name	Rank	Unit	Fate	Date	Place
Daltram, Amo		Mass.	Died	11-18-14	Dartmoor Prison
Damon, John	Private	13th Inf.	"	9-16-13	
Dandney, Hiram		Bladensburg	Killed	8-24-14	
Daniel, Martin	Private	Ky. Mil.	Died	1-1-15	
Daniel, John Moncure	Doctor	Hos.Surg.Ft.Geo.	"	10-7-13	
Daniel, Darnell	Private	Frenchtown	Killed	1-22-13	
Daniels, Samuel	"	9th Inf.	Died	--	
Danniels, N.	"	13th Inf.	"	9-15-13	
Darling, John	"	9th Inf.	Died	10-21-14	
Darr, Peter	"	17th Inf.	"	1-14-15	
Dashield, Levi	"	38th Inf.	"	2-12-14	
Daveroix, Jas. F.	"	16th Inf.	"	6-16-13	
Davey, John	"	20th Inf.	"	3-1-14	
David, Boyd	"	Lt. Art.	"	2-2-14	
David, John	"	Ky. Inf.	"	10-31-14	
Davidson, Robert M.	2 Lieut.	22nd Inf.	Killed	7-25-14	
Davis, Abraham	Q.M.	Saratoga	"	9-11-14	
Davis, Daniel	Brig.Gen		"	9-17-14	
Davis, Isaac	Private	Lt. Drag.	Died	6-8-13	
Davis, John	"	24th Inf.	"	Oct. 1814	
Davis, John		13th Inf.	"	11-29-13	
Davis, James	Private	11th Inf.	"	1-18-13	
Davis, James	Sailor	Mass	"	3-4-13	Chatham
Davis, Jon		Mass	"	2-25-15	
Davis, Solomon	Private	11th Inf.	"	8-10-14	
Davis, Stephen	"		"	7-23-13	Quebec Prison
Davis, Thomas	"	Essex	Killed	3-28-14	
Davis, Thomas Chiles	Surgeon	1st Reg.Ky.Vols	"	1-22-13	River Raisin
Davis, William		Lawrence	Died	9-10-13	
Davis, William	Private	1st Inf.	"	2-15-15	
Davis, Willis	"	20th Inf.	"	Oct. 1813	
Davison, Asabel	"	11th Inf.	"	4-2-13	
Dawes, James	"	33rd Inf.	Killed	10-27-13	
Dawson, Jno.	"	10th Inf.	Died	1-25-15	
Day, David	"	9th Inf.	"	3-18-13	
Day, James	Marine	Borer	Killed	9-11-14	
Day, William	Capt.	4th Reg.Inf.	Died	1-25-15	
Day, William	Private	12th Inf.	"	6-11-14	
Deady, Silas	"	13th Inf.	"	Dec. 1813	
Dean, L.	"	38th Inf.	"	3-21-14	
Deane, Jeremiah	"	15th Inf.	"	1-20-14	
Dearborn, Solomon	"		"	7-23-13	Quebec Prison
Dearborn, Thomas	"	21st Ing.	"	10-10-14	
Dearing, Jno.	"		"	9-28-13	Quebec Prison
Dearmond, John	"	Ky. Mil.	"	10-29-13	
Deberry, Benjamin	"	35th Inf.	"	12-2-14	
Deckar, Peter	"	22nd Inf.	"	12-25-14	
Decker, Christopher	"	6th Inf.	"	2-9-13	
DeFriend, Jno.	"		"	7-17-13	Quebec Prison
DeHunt, John	"	8th Inf.	"	10-21-14	
Delap, Wm.	"	Art.	"	Sept. 1914	
Delano, Benjamin		Mass.	"	3-30-15	
Delaney, John	"	22nd Inf.	"	1814	
DeLino de Chalmette Ignace	"	Orleans Vols.	"	2-10-15	

Name	Rank	Unit	Status	Date	Notes
Delphy, Richard	Midshipman	Argus	Killed	8-14-13	
Delshaver, Simon	Private	16th Inf.	Died	8-20-14	
Deming, Ebenezer	"	2nd Drag.	"	11-30-13	
Demwit, John	"	38th Inf.	"	12-18-13	
Denham, Silas	"	Mass.	"	11-14-14	Dartmoor Prison
Denice, Garret	"	N.J.Mil.1st Cav.	"	1-24-13	
Dennis, Thomas	"	15th Inf.	Killed	12-24-13	
Dennis, Wheatly	Lieut.	Co. 37th Rgt.	Died	1814	
Dennison, Joseph	Private	25th Inf.	"	11-7-13	
Denniss, Josh	"	15th Inf.	"	11-3-14	
Denny, David	"	O	"	1812	
Denny, I.	"	38th Inf.	"	4-18-14	
Denton, Thomas	"	6th Inf.	"	8-18-13	
Depass, George	"	14th Inf.	"	6-15-13	
Depriest, Austin	"	17th Inf.	"	12-18-14	
Deputnin, John	"	11th Inf.	"	4-20-13	
Derrickson, Elisha	"	16th Inf.	"	4-15-13	
Derrickson, Joseph	"	Art.	"	--	
Deshealds, Peter	"		"	10-20-13	Quebec Prison
Desmont, Henry	"	5th Inf.	"	8-21-14	
Deter, Adam	"	16th Inf.	Killed		At Fort George
Devin, William	"	15th Inf.	Died	8-11-13	
Devinas, John			"	4-12-15	Dartmoor Prison
Devoe, Isaac	"	25th Inf.	"	3-15-13	
Dexter, Eleazer	"	4th Inf.	"	1-18-14	
Deyen, Wm.	"	21st Inf.	"	8-24-13	
Diamond, William		R.I.-Mary.	"	1-10-14	Dartmoor Prison
Diamond, Wm.	"		"	1-23-15	Dartmoor Prison
Dibble, Tompkins	Private	13th Inf.	"	9-7-13	
Dickenson, Elisha	"	13th Inf.	"	2-8-15	
Dickerson, William Terry	"	7th U.S. Inf.	"	6-11-15	In N.Orleans Hos
Dickey, John	"	19th Inf.	"	Dec. 1812	
Dickey, John	"	31st Inf.	"	3-12-15	
Dicks, John	"	12th Inf.	"	1-1-14	
Dickson, Joseph	"		Killed	9-4-12	
Dilano, Amasa		R.I.	Died	11-18-14	Dartmoor Prison
Dillon, Robt.	Private	13th Inf.	"	11-11-13	
Dilton, William			"	5-10-14	Dartmoor Prison
Dishmore, James	Private	Ky. Mil.	"	3-20-15	
Diverance, James	Sailor	Mass.	"	7-5-13	Chatham
Dix, Timothy	Major	14th Reg.U.S.Inf.	"	10-14-13	
Dixon, John	Private	15th Inf.	Killed	11-4-13	
Dixon, N.	"	4th Inf.	Died	7-1-14	
Dixon, Robert	"	16th Inf.	"	8-1-14	
Dodds, Joseph	"	7th Inf.			
Dodds, Joseph			Killed	9-4-12	Ft. Harrison
Dodge, Iasiah	Private	13th Inf.	Died	2-6-15	
Dodge, Samuel	"	9th Inf.	"	12-22-13	
Dodge, William	"	9th Inf.	"	12-10-13	
Dodge, Zimmer	"	11th Inf.	"	11-11-13	
Doeph, Charles	"	7th Reg.Conn.Mil.	Killed	1-15-15	
Doherty, Anthony	"	16th Inf.	Died	11-11-13	
Dolphin, Edward	"	23rd Inf.	"	2-23-14	
Donaldson, Jas. L. Adj.			Killed	9-12-14	

Name	Rank	Unit	Status	Date	Location
Donaldson, James Lowrie	Lt. Adj.	27th Reg.	Killed	9-14-14	Battle-No. Point
Donaldson, A	"		"		Fort Strother
Donnald, James	Private	Ky. Mil.	Died	2-20-19	
Donnell	"	4th Inf.	"	1814	
Dononer, Wm.		Mass.	"	11-12-13	Dartmoor Prison
Dooley, Ephraim	1 Lieut		Killed	5-5-13	
Doolittle, Abraham	Private	11th Inf.	Died	8-22-14	
Door, Allen	"	9th Inf.	"	6-1-13	
Doran, Alexander	Lieut	Inf.E.Tenn.Mil	"	1814	
Dorman, William	Private	22nd Inf.	"	3-3-14	
Dornel, Saml.	"	17th Inf.	"	2-1-15	
Dorsell, Jededish	"	21st Inf.	"	5-20-15	
Dorsey, Patrick	"	45th Inf.	"	--	
Dotson, Thomas	"	Ky. Mil.	"	1-15-15	
Douchon, A.	Colonel	Tenn. Art.	"	1-22-14	
Dougherty, John	Private	Ky. Mil.	"	5-5-13	
Dougherty, Michl.	"	12th Inf.	"	8-9-13	
Dougherty. Anthony	"	15th Inf.	"	--	
Dougherty, Saml.	"	Lt. Drag.	"	10-15-14	
Douglas, Elijah	"	9th Inf.	"	Dec. 1813	
Douglass, James	"	21st Inf.	"	12-1-13	
Dowen, Oliver	"	6th Inf.	"	7-13-13	
Downey, Henry			Killed	1-22-13	Frenchtown
Downie, John H.	Sailor	Mass.	Died	4-27-13	Chatham
Doyal, Peter	Private	11th Inf.	"	9-16-14	
Drake, Darins	"	9th Inf.	"	May 1813	
Drane, Thomas	"	3rd Ky. Mil.	"	9-30-12	
Draton, Joseph	"	9th Inf.	Killed	11-11-13	
Dring, Samuel	"	41st Inf.	Died	1-22-14	
Dulton, James	"	15th Inf.	"	--	
Dungan, Benjamin	"	16th Inf.	Killed	6-6-13	
Dunham, David			Died	10-25-14	Dartmoor Prison
Duren, Joel	Private	1st Art.	"	10-7-12	
Durrett, William	"	3rd Ky. Mil.	"	11-23-12	
Dutcher, Charles	Corp.	22nd Inf.	"	3-28-14	
Duty, Benjamin	Private	30th Inf.	"	6-27-14	
Dwight, Francis H.	Marine		Killed	10-30-12	
Duboise, David	Private	23rd Inf.	Died	9-17-14	
Duckett, Richard	"	38th Inf.	"	9-8-14	
Dudd, Presley	"	20th Inf.	"	6-18-13	
Dudley,	Colonel		Killed		At Rapids
Dudley, Daniel	Private	4th Inf.	Died	5-28-13	
Dudley, Trueworthy	"	33rd Inf.	"	6-4-15	
Dudley, William	Colonel	13th Ky. Reg.	Killed	5-5-13	
Dulin, William	Private	24th Inf.	Died	1813	
Dumbotton, Benj.	"	6th Inf.	"	--	
Dunbar, Saml.	"	21st Inf.	"	--	
Duncan, John	"	3rd Art.	"	11-13-13	
Duneau, George	Corp.	17th Inf.	"	8-10-14	
Dunn, Gabriel	Private	Ky. Inf.	"	10-31-14	
Dunn, John	Seaman	Phila.	"	1814	Stapleton Prison
Dunn, Joshua	Private	12th Inf.	"	3-8-14	
Durand, George	"	41st Inf.	"	2-24-15	
Durham, Silas		Mass.	"	11-14-14	Dartmoor Prison

Duston, Ezekiel	Private	9th Inf.	Died	--	
Dutcher, Charles	"	23rd Inf.	"	2-28-14	
Duvall, Trueman	Captain	34th Rgt.	"	1814	
Dyehouse, Edward	Private	Ky. Mil.	"	9-26-13	
Dyer, Baldy	"	39th Inf.	"	Feb. 1815	
Dyer, Isaac	"		"	9-10-13	Quebec Prison
Dyer, John B.	"	14th Inf.	"	--	
Dyer, Jonathan		N.H.	2	3-11-15	Dartmoor Prison

Earens, Edward		N.J.	Died	1-6-15	Dartmoor Prison
Earl, Philip	Private	6th Inf.	"	9-19-13	
Earle, Amosa	"	4th Inf.	"	Oct. 1813	
Earle, Lewis		Essex	Killed	3-28-14	
East, Thomas	Private	Reg. La. Mil.	Died	2-16-15	
Eastburn, John	"	13th Inf.	"	--	
Easter, Stephen	"		"	6-28-13	Quebec Prison
Eastman, Chellis	"	11th Inf.	"	1-13-13	
Eastman, Henry	"	11th Inf.	"	--	
Eaton, Nathan	"	45th Inf.	"	12-26-14	
Eaton, Wm.	"		"	8-23-13	
Eccleston, Ichid	"	25th Inf.	"	12-26-14	
Eddy, George	"	5th Inf.	"	10-19-14	
Edgar, William		N.J.	"	1-26-14	Dartmoor Prison
Edmiston, John	Captain	7th Co.Rifles Ky.Mil	"	1-22-13	River Raisin
Edmonds, Robert	Private	23rd Inf.	"	--	
Edmonson, John	Captain		"	1-22-13	River Raisin
Edmonson, John	Private	Tenn. Mil.	Killed	1-22-13	River Raisin
Edmundson, John	Captain		"	1-22-13	River Raisin
Edsod, Wm.		N.J.-Hepsa	Died	1-27-14	Dartmoor Prison
Eggleston, Edward	Private	2nd Lt. Drag.	"	12-8-12	
Edwards, Benjamin	"	Lt. Drag.	"	12-24-12	
Edwards, Elisha	1 Lieut.	Ky. Vols	Killed	11-22-12	
Edwards, Robert	Captain	17th Inf.	"	1-22-13	
Edwards, Wm. W	Midshipman	Argus	"	8-14-13	
Eggert, Francis	Seaman	Argus	"	8-14-13	
Eldridge, Joseph C.	1 Lieut.	13th Inf.	"	7-8-13	
Eldridge, Levi	Private	9th Inf.	Died	--	
Elias, Edmonds	"	12th Inf.	"	10-13-13	
Elingwood, Wm.	Sailor	Mass.	"	5-19-13	Chatham
Eliott, Robt.	Private	2nd Art.	"	4-18-14	
Elliot, James	"	9th Inf.	"	1-4-14	

Elliott, George	Private	6th Inf.	Died	10-12-14	
Elliott, Gosberg	"	O	"	1813	
Elliott, James	"	Ky. Inf.	"	5-5-13	
Elliott, William	"	21st Inf.	"	3-7-14	
Elliott, William	"	3rd Pa. Mil.	"	2-10-13	
Ellis, Daniel	"	11th Inf.	"	4-10-13	
Ellis, Giles	"	25th Inf.	"	7-22-14	
Ells, Samuel	"	27th Inf.	"	11-7-14	
Elroy, Benjamin C.	"	3rd Art.	"	10-8-13	
Elum, Robert	"	10th Inf.	"	4-2-14	
Elvel, B.		Mass.	"	3-10-15	Ashburton
Elvell, Benjamin	Sailor	Mass.	"	4-18-13	Chatham
Emerson, Jonathan	Private	9th Inf.	"	12-22-13	
Emerson, Samuel F.	"	11th Inf.	"	12-24-13	
English, John	"	11th Inf.	"	9-16-13	
English, Thomas	"	2nd Art.	"	12-11-13	
Enns, Sylvanus	"	U.S. Art.	"	6-7-13	
Eustis, Thomas	"	3rd Art.	"	1813	
Evans, Jacob	"	45th Inf.	"	2-17-15	
Evans, Edward		N.Y.	"	1-6-15	Dartmoor Prison
Evans, John	Midshipman	Chesapeake	Killed	6-1-13	
Evans, Robert	Private	34th Inf.	Died	10-12-14	
Evans, Thomas		Chesapeake	Killed	6-1-13	
Evans, William R.	Private	29th Inf.	Died	11-18-14	
Evans, William R.	"	10th Inf.	"	9-29-14	
Evans, William R.	"	Lt. Art.	"	12-4-14	
Everheart, Saml.	"	Art.	"	--	
Evin, William			"	3-14-15	Dartmoor Prison
Evins, Robert	Corp.	34th Inf.	"	10-12-14	
Evins, William K.	Private	29th Inf.	"	9-16-14	
Eyres, John	"	12th Inf.	"	5-2-14	

Fagan, Terence	Private	Lt. Drag.	Died	10-10-14
Fairchild, John	"	12th Inf.	"	11-30-13
Fairfield, William	"	11th Inf.	"	8-3-14
Fairlong, Mordetti	"	17th Inf.	"	1-21-14
Fallier, George	"	39th Rgt.	"	9-19-13
Fango, Matthew	Gunner	Surprise	Drowned	4-5-15
Farber, Henry	Private	14th Inf.	Died	11-11-13
Farmer, Gray B.	"	Ky. Mil.	"	2-16-15
Farmlain, Philip	"	10th Inf.	"	12-1-13

Name	Rank	Unit	Fate	Date	Notes
Farnum, Joel	Private	11th Inf.	Died	3-4-14	
Farrell, Archibald	"	6th Inf.	"	1-12-13	
Fash, Nehemiah	"	5th Inf.	"	1-20-15	
Fawells, Arthur	"	18th Inf.	"	12-26-14	
Faunce, Caleb	"	40th Inf.	"	4-24-14	
Fegin, Wm.	"	1st Inf.	"	12-21-14	
Felton,	Ensign		Killed	8-4-14	
Fennel, William		N.H.	Died	1-23-13	Dartmoor Prison
Fenning, Chas.	Private		"	6-5-13	Quebec Prison
Ferguson, James, Sr.	"	Pa. Mil.	"	4-30-13	
Ferguson, Samuel	"	7th U.S. Inf.	"	1-4-14	
Ferree, Joel	Captain	NW. Army	Killed	10-25-14	on U.S. Frigate
Ferree, Joel	Lt. Col.	2nd Brig.Pa.Mil	Died	4-9-13	
Ferrell, John	Private	O	"	1812	
Ferry, Dennis	"	15th Inf.	"	4-27-13	
Ferza, William		N.Y.	"	2-25-14	Dartmoor Prison
Field, Jesse		Me.	"	11-12-13	Dartmoor Prison
Field, Joseph	Corp.	Va. Mil.	"	Mar. 1815	
Field, Stephen	Private	15th Inf.	"	1-24-15	
Fields, G.	Corp.	1st Rifles	"	--	
Figg, John	Ensign	Ky. Mil.	"	12-19-14	
Filbrick, David	Private	33rd Inf.	"	10-1-14	
Filer, Horace	"	25th Inf.	"	11-18-13	
Filkins, William	Sgt.	7th U.S. Inf.	"	5-2-14	
Finch, Jeremiah B.	Private	15th Inf.	"	1-6-13	
Finley, John	Seaman	Argus	Killed	8-14-13	
Finley, Wm.	"	Argus	"	8-14-13	
Finney, Elihu	Private		Died	8-10-13	Quebec Prison
Fish, Bolton	"	9th Inf.	"	7-25-14	
Fish, Daniel	"	23rd Inf.	"	Jan. 1814	
Fish, Elisha	"	25th Inf.	"	8-28-14	
Fish, Levin	"	12th Inf.	"	--	
Fishback, John	"	9th Inf.	"	11-26-14	
Fisher, John	"	11th Inf.	"	8-30-14	
Fisher, John	Mate	Ticonderoga	Killed	9-11-14	
Fisher, John	Private	Co.15th Reg.Pa.Mil.	Died	11-19-15	
Fisher, Thomas	"	11th Inf.	"	7-25-14	
Fitch, William	"	Lt. Art.	"	12-1-13	
Fitzjarrell, Silas	"	Ky. Mil.	"	9-28-13	
Fitzpatrick, James	"	17th Inf.	"	11-10-13	
Flanagan, William	"	10th Inf.	"	10-10-14	
Flandrew, Geo.	"	25th Inf.	"	12-28-13	
Flansburgh, Jacob	"	N.Y. Mil.	"	12-13-15	
Flanders, Joseph	"	4th Inf.	"	11-28-13	
Flansley, Lewis	"	20th Inf.	"	3-8-14	
Fleming, James	"	15th Inf.	"	11-3-14	
Fleming, Patrick	"	19th Inf.	"	1814	
Fleming, Patrick	"	17th Inf.	"	11- 6-14	
Flemming, David	"	17th Inf.	"	1-14-15	
Flenner, John	"	3rd Rifles	"	10-24-14	
Fletcher, Thomas	"	Ky. Mil.	"	10-29-13	
Fletcher, Wm.		Mass	"	--	Dartmoor Prison
Flint, Surrell	"	9th Inf.	"	6-5-13	
Flowers, Andrew	"	14th Inf.	"	2-25-14	

Flynn, Peter	Private	4th Rifles	Died	8-9-14	
Fogerty, Archibald		Mass.	"	3-18-15	Dartmoor Prison
Foldger, James	Sailor	Essex	Killed	3-28-14	
Folin, Benjamin	Private	Ky. Mil.	Died	8-10-13	
Foller, Wm.	Sailor	Mass.	"	1-27-13	Chatham
Follinsbee, Samuel	Private	4th Inf.	"	11-4-13	
Foot, Nathan	"	25th Inf.	"	12-26-13	
Foquet, Thomas			"	3-18-14	Dartmoor Prison
Forbes, Enoch	Private	18th Inf.	"	9-18-14	
Forbes, Sandy	Seaman	Globe	Killed	11-1-13	
Force, Baldwin	Private	6th Inf.	Died	11-22-14	
Ford, Andy	"	7th U.S. Inf.	"	5-26-14	
Ford, John C.D.	"	2nd Art.	"	1-6-13	
Ford, Joseph	"	7th U.S. Inf.	"	5-7-14	
Ford, Levi G.	Captain	8th Cav. Dist.	"	1814	
Ford, William	Private	38th Inf.	"	12-10-14	
Foreman, Robert	"	27th Inf.	"	--	
Forman, William	Sailor	N.H.	"	4-12-14	Chatham
Forsyth, Benjamin	Lt.Col.	U.S. Rifles	Killed	6-28-14	At Adletown,L.C.
Fortune, Samuel	Sailor	Navy	"	10-6-12	
Fosburgh, Russell	Private	1st Art.	Died	3-16-14	
Foster, Enos	"	9th Inf.	"	7-25-14	
Foster, Joel	"	10th Inf.	"	9-22-14	
Foster, Nathl.	"		"	8-25-13	Quebec Prison
Foster, Richard	"	24th Inf.	"	12-19-13	
Foster, Samuel	"	3rd Art.	"	5-10-13	
Fought, Jacob	"	15th Inf.	"	4-15-14	
Fountain, James	"	35th Inf.	"	2-4-15	
Fowler, Alexander	"	Lt. Drag.	"	7-2-14	
Fowler, Joshua		Mass.	"	11-30-13	Dartmoor Prison
Fowler, Morris	Private	9th Inf.	"	12-9-13	
Fowler, Samuel	"	7th U.S. Inf.	"	4-22-14	
Fowler, Thomas	"	Ky. Mil.	"	2-2-15	
Fowler, Thomas	"	16th Inf.	"	11-4-12	
Fox, John	"	13th Inf.	"	4-15-14	
Foy, Darby	"	8th Inf.	"	2-18-14	
Foy, Jacob	"	45th Inf.	"	9-30-14	
Framel, William	"	8th Inf.	"	9-16-14	
Frances, Thomas	"	Ky. Mil.	"	9-28-13	
Francis, D.	Seaman	R.I.	"	June 1814	Stapleton Prison
Francis, John		Va.	"	4-16-15	
Francisco, Israel	Private	6th Inf.	"	--	
Franklin,	Corp.	1st Rifles	"	--	
Franklin, John	Private	29th Inf.	"	7-6-14	
Franklin, S. W.	Lieut.	43rd Rgt.	"	1814	
Frask, Elias	Private	34th Inf.	"	9-20-14	
Frazer, John	Seaman	Surprise	Drowned	4-5-15	
Frazer, Philip	Cook	SS Alligator	Died	7-1-14	
Frazier, Elijah	Private	8th Inf.	"	8-7-14	
Frederich, Lewi	"	10th Inf.	"	1814	
Freear, Robert	"	10th Inf.	"	1-18-14	
Freely, Henry		Pa.	"	1-20-14	Dartmoor Prison
Freeman, Scotto	"	21st Inf.	"	--	
Frelitch, Henry		Pa.	"	12-23-13	Dartmoor Prison

French, Joseph	Private	Ky. Mil.	Died	2-21-15	
Frick, David	"	5th Inf.	"	10-4-14	
Frost, Phinehas	"		"	10-22-13	Quebec Prison
Frost, W	"	1st Rifles	"	--	
Frozer, Samuel W.	"	4th Inf.	"	4-5-13	
Fry, Asa	"	11th Inf.	"	9-14-14	
Fry, John, 3rd	"	Pa. Mil.	"	12-28-14	
Fry, John	"	33rd Inf.	"	12-29-14	
Fry, John	"	34th Inf.	"	12-11-14	
Fry, Thomas	"	11th Inf.	"	9-14-14	
Frye, Isaac	"	11th Inf.	"	9-14-14	
Frye, Theophilus	"	21st Inf.	"	3-6-15	
Fryman, Henry	"	17th Inf.	"	--	
Fulford, James		N.C.	"	1-27-14	Dartmoor Prison
Fuller, Calvin	Private	11th Inf.	"	4-19-13	
Fuller, George	Sgt.	14th Inf.	"	7-28-13	
Fuller, Hubbell S.	Private	23rd Inf.	"	--	
Fuller, Jeremiah	"	11th Inf.	"	8-15-14	
Fuller, John	"	23rd Inf.	"	3-8-14	
Fuller, Timothy	"	11th Inf.	"	5-13-13	
Fulton, David	"	6th Inf.	"	4-27-13	
Fulton, James	Sgt.	22nd Inf.	"	--	
Fundy, Anthony	Sailor	N.Y.	"	3-27-13	Chatham
Funk, John	Private	22nd Inf.	"	6-1-14	
Funk, John Musser	Lieut.	U.S.N.	"	10-25-12	
Furlong, William	Private	3rd Div.Md.Mil.	"	11-23-14	at N.Point, Md.
Furnal, Wm.		N.H.	"	1-23-14	Dartmoor Prison
Gaddis, James	Private	22nd Inf.	Died	12-14-12	
Gadeau, Lewis	"	27th Inf.	"	10-23-14	
Gailon, Jno.		N.C.	"	12-3-14	Dartmoor Prison
Gaines, James	Private	U.S. Inf.	"	11-24-14	
Gaines, Thomas	"	2nd Rfls.	"	2-2-15	
Gale, John	"	4th Inf.	"	5-7-14	
Galloway, John	"	41st Inf.	"	5-31-14	
Gamble, Peter	Lieut.	Saratoga	Killed	9-11-14	
Gamble, Stansbury	Lieut.	35th Rgt.	Died	1815	
Gannon, Harten	Private	22nd Inf.	"	9-10-14	
Gardner, Diark	"	6th Inf.	"	2-13-13	
Gardner, Francis	Sailor	R.I. Rambler	"	11-4-14	Dartmoor Prison
Gardner, George	Seaman	Argus	Killed	8-14-13	

Name	Rank	Unit	Fate	Date	Location
Gardner, Jeremiah		R.I.	Died	3-4-15	Dartmoor Prison
Gardner, John	Private	17th Inf.	"	1-22-13	
Gardner, Z.	"	9th Inf.	"	7-24-13	
Garlack, Elias	"	13th Inf.	"	10-13-12	
Garrabrantz, Peter I.	"	15th Rifles	"	12-1-13	
Garren, Nathaniel		Enterprise	Killed	9-5-13	
Garret, Caleb	Private	10th Inf.	Died	3-21-14	
Gasgiline, Thomas		W.I.	"	4-19-14	Dartmoor Prison
Gaston, Hugh	Private	1st Rfls.	"	5-7-14	
Gates, Pearly	Captain	N.Y. Mil.	"	2-27-13	
Gauslin, Alex	Private	20th Inf.	"	8-3-13	
Gaylor, John		N.C.	"	12-3-14	Dartmoor Prison
Gedman, James		N.H.	"	2-17-15	Dartmoor Prison
Geralds, Thomas	Private	30th Inf.	"	4-8-14	
Gerles, Charles	"		Killed	1-22-13	at Frenchtown
German, John	"	10th Inf.	Died	11-5-14	
Gerrald, William	"	21st Inf.	"	12-13-14	
Getchel, Nehemiah	"	33rd Inf.	"	10-31-13	
Gibson, Charles, Jr.	"	Pa. Mil.	"	9-18-14	
Gibson, James	Colonel	Asst.Insp.Gen.	Killed	9-17-14	
Gibson, Jordan		Ky. Mil.	Died	1-4-15	
Gibson, Richard	Private	10th Inf.	"	10-10-13	
Gibson, Thos.	Corp.	Art. Reg.	"	9-11-14	
Gibson, William	Private	U.S. Inf.	"	12-31-14	
Gibson, Wm.		N.Y.	"	10-22-14	Dartmoor Prison
Giddis, Jeremiah	Private	3rd Art.	"	10-30-12	
Gilchrist, Robt.	Captain		Killed	8-5-12	
Gilbert, Isaac	Private	25th Inf.	Died	11-23-12	
Gilbert, William	"	17th Inf.	"	9-4-14	
Gilfillom, Alexander Dr.	Surgeon	to Black Rock	Drowned	6-17-15	
Gill, Thomas (boy)		USN Borer	Died	9-11-14	
Gilles, John	Private	Lt. Drag.	"	10-23-14	
Gilliam, Samuel	"	65th Reg.Va.Mil.	"	4-25-15	
Gilky, Thomas	"	Ky. Mil.	"	1-4-15	
Gill, John	"	Ky. Mil.	"	2-28-15	
Gilliland, William	"	22nd Inf.	"	8-7-13	
Gilson, Thomas	"	Pa. Mil.	"	11-19-13	
Girton, Jonathan	"	Art.	"	12-31-14	
Girton, Thos.	"		"	8-23-13	Quebec Prison
Gladden, Wm.	"	22nd Inf.	"	2-20-15	
Gladding, Jonathan		R.I.	"	3-14-15	Dartmoor Prison
Glass, Reuben		Mass.	"	May 1813	Dartmoor Prison
Gleffan, Thomas	"	19th Inf.	"	10-22-14	
Glidden, Winthrop	"	21st Inf.	"	12-27-13	
Gload, Elnathan	"	13th Inf.	"	4-28-13	
Glover, Joshua	"	9th Inf.	"	5-29-13	
Goddard, John	"	20th Inf.	"	5-1-13	
Goddrich, H.Y.C.	"		"	10-20-13	Quebec Prison
Goff, Esaw	"	12th Inf.	"	12-18-13	
Gofarth, John	"	7th Inf.	"	7-17-14	
Golden, David	"	6th Inf.	"	1-25-13	
Goldsbury, William	"	Vol. Vt. Mil.	"	5-12-15	
Goles, John	"	4th Inf.	"	5-7-14	
Gomans, James	"	11th Inf.	"	2-19-13	

Goodall, John	Private	29th Inf.	Died	1-15-15	
Goodenough, David	"	101st Reg.N.Y.Mil.	"	10-9-14	
Goodenough, Henry	"	11th Inf.	"	2-11-15	
Goodenough, Liberty	"	11th Inf.	"	1-22-13	
Goodenow, Hezekiah	"	11th Inf.	"	11-15-14	
Goodnow, Elisha	"	Lt. Drag.	"	--	
Goodnow, Eli	"		"	5-13-13	Quebec Prison
Goodrich, Allen	"	13th Inf.	Killed		at Queenstown
Goodrich, Val R.	Captain	11th Inf.	"	7-25-14	
Goodrich	"	11th Inf.	Died	11-11-13	
Goodwill, James	Private	23rd Inf.	"	6-8-13	
Goodwin, Amaziah	"	Art.	"	10-15-12	
Goodwin, Charles	"	38th Inf.	"	1-10-15	
Goodwin, Peter	"	Art. Reg.	"	9-11-14	
Goodwin, Tristram	"	9th Inf.	"	12-27-13	
Gordin, John, Jr.	"	21st Inf.	"	3-15-15	
Gordon, Isaac	"	27th Inf.	"	--	
Gordon, Thomas	"	15th Inf.	"	10-15-12	
Gordon, William	"	21st Inf.	"	8-5-13	
Gordon, William	"	14th Inf.	"	11-20-12	
Goselin, Thos.	"	Fr.W.I.	"	4-29-14	Dartmoor Prison
Goseline, Richard	"	13th Inf.	"	12-1-12	
Gould, Jno.	"	11th Inf.	"	10-30-14	
Gould, Jonathan	"	3rd Art.	"	3-24-13	
Gould, John	"	45th Inf.	"	11-23-14	
Gould, John	"	11th Inf.	"	11-11-14	
Gould, John	"	9th Inf.	"	11-18-13	
Gould, John	"	11th Inf.	"	Nov. 13	
Gould, John	"	21st Inf.	"	8-28-14	
Gould, Levi	"	23rd Inf.	"	9-30-14	
Gawe, William	"	Ky. Mil.	"	6-19-13	
Goyer, Denny L.	"	15th Inf.	"	7-15-14	
Grace, Henry	"	Ky. Mil.	"	2-8-15	
Graham, Benj.	"	3rd Art.	"	12-12-13	
Graindy, Amos	Sailor	Mass.	"	5-18-14	Chatham
Grandy, Eri	Private	29th Inf.	"	6-26-14	
Granger,	"	29th Inf.	"	2-26-14	
Grant, Godfrey	"	41st Inf.	"	--	
Grant, Jeremiah	Captain	High Flyer	Killed Oct 1812		
Grant, John	Sailor	Chesapeake	"	6-1-13	
Grant, Robt. N.	Private	20th Inf.	Died	12-31-12	
Grant, William, III	"	Ky. Mil.	"	2-20-14	
Grapevine, Fred	"	5th Inf.	"	--	
Graves, Jeffery	Sailor	Alligator	"	7-1-14	
Graves, Lebins	Private	14th N.Y. Vols	"	9-25-14	
Graves, Thos. C.	1 Lieut.	17th Inf.	Killed	1-22-13	
Gray, A.	Captain	Dep.Q.M.General	Died	--	
Gray, Danl.	Private	42nd Inf.	"	1-11-15	
Gray, James	"	13th Inf.	"	9-14-13	
Grayham, William	"	Ky. Mil.	"	1-28-15	
Greely, Samuel	"	23rd Inf.	"	July 1813	
Green, Eben	"	9th Inf.	"	4-8-14	
Green, Edward	"	Art.	"	10-7-12	
Green, Elijah	"		"	7-23-13	Quebec Prison

Name	Rank	Unit		Fate	Date	Notes
Green, Francis	Sailor	Essex		Killed	3-28-14	
Green, James	Private	Ky. Mil.		Died	1-19-15	
Green, James B.	Sailor	Va.		"	6-6-13	
Green, John R.	Private	8th Inf.		"	5-20-14	
Greenes, Thos.		Mass.		"	2-27-15	Dartmoor Prison
Greenlief, E. G.	Private	31st Inf.		"	9-20-14	
Greer, Levin W.	Lieut.Ga.	43rd Inf.		Killed	11-29-13	
Gregory, Read	Private	25th Inf.		Died	12-10-12	
Gregory, Stephen	"	16th Inf.		"	9-21-14	
Gregory, Thomas	"	1st Rfls.		"	1814	
Gregory, Walter	"	Ky. Mil.		"	8-26-13	
Grey, Duncan	"	14th N.Y. Vols.		"	10-25-14	
Griffin, James	"	11th Inf.		"	8-1-14	
Griffin, Lewis	"	2nd Art.		"	8-15-13	
Griffin, Theophelus	"	4th Inf.		"	9-28-14	
Griffin, Thos.	"	9th Inf.		"	4-10-14	
Griffith, Joshua	"	32nd Rgt.		"	1813	
Griffith, Samuel	Captain	U.S. Vols.3rd Inf.		"	1815	In Mo.
Griffith, Samuel	Surgeons Mate	11th Rgt.		"	1814	
Griffith, Sylvanus	Lieut.	10th Rgt.		"	9-20-13	
Griggory, Stephen	Private	16th Inf.		"	9-21-14	
Grimes, James	"	11th Inf.		"	9-19-14	
Grimes, Thomas	"	16th Inf.		"	10-12-14	
Grisold, Jas.	"			"	1-7-13	Quebec Prison
Grissam, James	"	Ky. Inf.		"	10-31-14	
Griswold, Elisha	"	11th Inf.		"	3-6-14	
Griswold, Josiah	"	Vols. 6		"	--	
Grossman, Samuel	"	2nd Art.		"	1-4-14	
Grout, Demil	"	23rd Inf.		"	7-6-13	
Grover, Peter	"	13th Inf.		"	1-15-15	
Groves, George	"	21st Inf.		Killed	11-11-13	
Groves, Robert	Sailor	Wasp		"	10-18-12	
Groves, Thomas		Mass.		Died	2-23-15	Dartmoor Prison
Growler	"	Mass.		"	4-24-14	Chatham
Gudman, Franc	"	N.H.		"	2-17-15	Dartmoor Prison
Guines, James	Private	28th Inf.		"	--	
Gun, Josiah		Mass.	Mil.)"		2-23-15	Dartmoor Prison
Gunn, John	Private	2nd Inf.Reg.W.Tenn.)"		Nov.	1815	
Gurtrie, Jas.	"	22nd Inf.		"	12-5-14	
Guthum, James	"	22nd Inf.		"	12-5-14	
Guy, Jno.	"	23rd Inf.		"	9-7-14	
Gwinn, Josiah		Mass.		"	2-22-15	Dartmoor Prison

Hackenburg, Adam	Private	22nd Inf.	Died	9-2-14	
Hadley, Amos	"	9th Inf.	"	8-6-14	
Hadison, Silas	"	N.C.	"	12-4-14	
Hagan, Isaac	"	14th Inf.	"	1-12-15	
Hagerman, Isaac	"	22nd Inf.	"	12-13-13	
Hakes, Jesse	"	23rd Inf.	"	May 1813	
Hale, H.	Captain		Killed	9-17-14	
Hale, Horace	"	11th Inf.	"	9-17-14	
Hale, James W.	Musician	Eagle	"	9-11-14	
Hall, Daniel	Private	3rd Art.	Died	--	
Hall, James	"	22nd Inf.	"	--	
Hall, Frederick	Sailor	Essex	Killed	3-28-14	
Hall, John	Private	22nd Inf.	Died	1-24-14	
Hall, Levi	"	25th Inf.	"	12-15-13	
Hall, Lyman	"	11th Inf.	"	10-26-14	
Hall, Robert	"	Lt. Drag.	"	1-3-15	
Hall, Simon	"	10th Inf.	"	10-26-14	
Hall, Thomas			"	4-18-15	Dartmoor Prison
Hallett, George	Sailor	Essex	Killed	3-28-14	
Hallett, Nathan	Private	15th Inf.	Died	Dec. 1813	
Hallman, Stephen	"	19th Inf.	"	--	
Halsey, Her	"	13th Inf.	"	10-29-12	
Ham, John	"	Art.	"	7-5-13	
Hambert, Jacob	"		Killed	9-14-14	
Hambright, Henry, Jr.	"	5th Inf.	Died	4-16-15	
Hames, Nathan	"	16th Inf.	"	7-29-13	
Hamilton, Lt.	Sailor	U.S.S.President	Killed	1-5-14	
Hamm, James	Private	Ky. Mil.	Died	6-20-13	
Hammilton, Thomas	"	15th Inf.	"	7-22-13	
Hammon, John	"	Ky. Mil.	"	12-14-14	
Hammon, Jonathan	"	42nd Inf.	"	11-30-14	
Hammon, William	"	22nd Inf.	"	9-11-14	
Hammond, Abner	"	6th Inf.	"	12-25-13	
Hampton, Hutten	"	16th Inf.	"	11-17-14	
Hampton, Walter	"	16th Inf.	"	11-18-14	
Hankerson, J.	"	4th Inf.	"	8-16-14	
Hankins, George	"	1st Rifles	"	10-15-16	
Hanks, Porter	Lieut.	Art.	Killed	8-16-12	
Hanley, Jacob		Mass.	Died	2-5-15	Dartmoor Prison
Hanna, Williams	Private	Art.	"	--	
Hannah, William	"	5th Inf.	"	9-29-14	
Hannemen, Earl		Champ.Squad	Killed	9-11-14	
Hanson, Peter	Seaman	Saratoga	"	9-11-14	
Hanson, Thomas	Marine	USS Constitution	"	12-29-12	
Hardesty, Clemons	Private	Ky. Mil.	Died	12-19-14	
Hardesty, George	"	17th Inf.	"	2-11-15	
Hardgroves,	"	8th Inf.	"	June 1814	
Harding, C	"	1st Rifles	"	--	
Hardison, Silas		N.C.	"	12-4-14	Dartmoor Prison
Hardy, Isaac	Sailor	Lawrence	Killed	9-10-13	
Harkins, Patrick	Private	15th Inf.	Died	6-4-14	
Harlow, Josiah	"	25th Inf.	"	1-12-15	
Hardy, Ebenezer	"	9th Inf.	Killed	11-14-13	
Hardy, Isaac	Seaman	Niagara	"	12-31-13	
Hardy, Isaac	"	Niagara	"	9-10-13	

Name	Rank	Unit	Status	Date	Notes
Hardy, John	Corporal	35th Inf.	Died	2-18-15	
Hardy, John	Private	12th Inf.	"	--	
Harman, Henry	"	US Inf.	"	11-4-14	
Harland, Jesse	"		Killed	12-31-13	
Harlow, Jabez	Sgt.	9th Inf.	Died	11-20-13	
Harnsby, Asa	Private	5th Inf.	"	10-26-14	
Harradon, Elisha	"		"	7-15-13	Quebec Prison
Harrall, William	Lieut.	Ky. Mil.	"	2-23-15	
Harress, Daniel	Private	8th Inf.	"	Nov. 1813	
Harress, Simeon		N.Y.	"	3-5-15	Dartmoor Prison
Harress, William		N.H.	"	11-24-14	Dartmoor Prison
Harriman, M.	Private	4th Inf.	"	11-1-14	
Harriman, Moses	"	4th Inf.	"	10-26-14	
Harrington, James	Drummer	27th N.Y. Mil.	"	1814	
Harrington, Stephen	Captain	O. Mil.	"	7-11-12	
Harris, Francis	Corporal	13th Inf.	"	Oct. 1812	
Harris, Jacob	Private	7th US Inf.	"	1-16-14	
Harris, Job	"	21st Inf.	"	--	
Harris, John	"	11th Inf.	"	1-27-15	
Harris, Nelson	"	Ga. Mil.	"	1815	
Harris, Simen		N.Y.	"	3-5-14	Dartmoor Prison
Harris, Tracy	Private	11th Inf.	"	5-18-13	
Harris, Wm.		N.H.	"	11-24-14	Dartmoor Prison
Harrison, Carlisle	2 Lieut.	28th Inf.	Killed	7-16-14	
Harrison,	Lieut.		"	7-16-14	near Malden
Harrison, Ezell,	Private	Ky. Mil.	Died	12-28-14	
Harrison, John	1 Lieut.	Globe	Killed	11-1-13	
Harrison, Wm.	Sgt.	6th Ky. Mil.	Died	12-8-12	
Harriss, Daniel	Private	9th U.S. Inf.	"	5-28-13	Sacketts Harbor
Harshel, John	"	6th Ky. Mil.	"	12-5-12	
Hart, Asa	Seaman	Globe	"	11-1-13	
Hart, Barney	"	U.S. Const.	"	12-29-12	
Hart, James	Private	Mass. Mil.	"	11-28-14	
Hart, James	"	N.Y.	"	7-8-14	Dartmoor Prison
Hart, John	"	6th Inf.	"	6-16-13	
Hart, Joseph		Courier	"	1814	Dartmoor Prison
Hart, N G S	Captain		Killed	1-22-13	
Hart, Patrick	Private	8th Inf.	Died	12-6-13	
Hart, William	Sailor		"	2-14-14	Chatham
Hartford, Elias	Soldier		"	1-6-15	Dartmoor Prison
Hartford, Elijah		St.Thomas-Inf.	"	1-6-15	Dartmoor Prison
Hartman, Wm.	Private	2nd Art.	"	11-20-13	
Harvey, Thos.	Seaman	Alligator	"	7-1-14	
Haskell, John	Private	9th Inf.	Killed	7-23-13	
Haskell, William		Champ Squad	"	9-11-14	
Haskel, William	Private	40th Inf.	Died	3-31-15	
Haskins, Levi	"	25th Inf.	"	10-7-14	
Haslett, Moses	"	7th US Inf.	"	4-2-14	
Hass, John	"	8th Inf.	"	12-19-14	
Hastings, Benj.	"	21st Inf.	"	12-11-12	
Hastings, Joseph	"	25th Inf.	"	9-19-14	
Hatch, Jonathan	"	Art.	"	1-17-15	
Hatch, Robert	Pilot	Alligator	"	2-6-14	
Hatch, Timothy	Private	11th Inf.	"	4-24-13	
Hatfield, John	Midshipman	Madison	Killed	4-24-13	

Hathaway, Presley B.	Mate	Alligator	Died	7-1-14	
Hathaway, Thomas	Private	9th Inf.	Killed	12-22-13	
Hatch, Timothy	"	11th Inf.	Died	4-24-13	
Hatcher, Charles	"	25th Inf.	"	10-7-14	
Hawkes,	"	20th Inf.	"	8-18-13	
Hawkins, Jonathan	"	10th Inf.	"	12-23-13	
Hawkins, Philip	"	5th Inf.	"	4-12-14	
Harwood, John			Killed	4-6-15	Dartmoor Prison
Hay, William	Private	3rd Art	Died	12-4-13	
Haycock, Joseph		Me	"	3-20-15	Dartmoor Prison
Haynes, John	Private		"	11-12-14	
Hayth, Elisha	"	19th Inf.	"	10-15-14	
Hayward, George	"	14th Inf.	"	1814	
Haywood, John	Seaman		Killed	4-6-15	Dartmoor Prison
Haywood, John		Va	Died	4-6-15	Dartmoor Prison
Hazard, Ezekiel	Private		"	2-25-13	Quebec Prison
Hazen, Benjamin		Essex	Killed	3-28-14	
Heacock,	Private	4th Inf.	Died	8-28-14	
Head, Samuel	Sailor	N.Y.	"	3-29-14	Chatham
Heading,	Private	25th Inf.	"	7-16-13	
Healy, William	"	11th Inf.	"	12-6-14	
Heard, Timothy	"	9th Inf.	"	1814	
Hearsey, Bela	"	3rd Art.	"	8-30-13	
Heart, Jos.		N.Y.	"	7-8-14	Dartmoor Prison
Heath, Amos	Private	21st Inf.	"	1-8-14	
Heath, John, Sr.	"	3rd Rfls.	"	9-21-14	
Heath, Thomas	"	31st Inf.	"	4-19-15	
Heaton, Jesse	"	25th Inf.	"	7-27-13	
Heaton, Joseph	Marine	Eagle	Killed	9-11-14	
Heaton, Wm. S.	1 Lieut.	11th Inf.	Died	11-11-13	
Hedding, Amos	Private	25th Inf.	"	7-25-13	
Hedgepeth, Noah	"	10th Inf.	"	6-2-14	
Hedges, John	"	4th Inf.	"	2-25-15	
Hedges, Saml.	"	4th Rfls.	"	1-2-15	
Helms, Abraham	"	12th Inf.	"	5-14-14	
Hemenway, James	"	9th Inf.	"	12-20-13	
Hemphill, Saml.	"	16th Inf.	"	--	
Henderson, Alexander		N.Y.	"	12-29-14	Dartmoor Prison
Henderson, James	Colonel	--	Killed	12-28-14	
Henderson, James	Private	1st Inf.	Died	10-28-14	
Henderson, John	"	9th Inf.	"	--	
Henderson, Robert	"	16th Inf.	"	7-18-13	
Hendy, Jacob	Com.	--	"	2-5-14	Dartmoor Prison
Henley, Edward	Private	9th Inf.	"	9-17-14	
Henley, Samuel M.	"	7th Inf.	"	6-30-14	
Henry, Adigo		Pa.	"	12-23-13	Dartmoor Prison
Henry, Archibald	Private	Ky. Mil.	"	3-13-14	
Henry, James		N.Y.	"	7-3-14	Dartmoor Prison
Henry, Jason		N.Y.	"	7-3-14	Dartmoor Prison
Hensdale, Strong	Private	Lt. Art.	"	12-11-13	
Hepwood, John	Sgt.	Rifles	"	11-23-13	
Hermain, Isaac		Me.	"	11-9-14	
Herrick, Eli	Corp.	--	"	7-30-13	Quebec Prison
Herrick, Samuel	Private	9th Inf.	"	3-17-13	
Herriman, Moses	"	4th Inf.	"	10-26-14	

Herves, William	Private	N.Y. Vols	Died	8-4-14	
Hess, William	"	Tenn. Mil.	"	7-30-15	
Hetrope, James		Mass.	"	11-11-14	Dartmoor Prison
Hewes, Wm.	Private	25th Inf.	"	8-4-15	
Hewlet, Gold	"	10th Inf.	"	10-17-14	
Heymer, Dav.	"	41st Inf.	"	3-8-15	
Hickman, Pascal	Captain	Frenchtown	Killed	1-22-13	
Hickok, Amos	Private	25th Inf.	Died	9-15-13	
Hicock, Oliver	Corp.	11th Inf.	Killed	10-3-13	
Hicks, John	Private	4th Ga. Inf.	"	5-6-15	New Orleans
Hicks, Levi	"	11th Inf.	Died	1-26-13	
Hicks, Richard	"	Ky. Mil.	"	2-21-15	
Hicks, Thomas	"	6th Inf.	"	--	
Higginbottom, Moses	"	US Inf.	"	11-22-14	
Hildreth, Peter	"	11th Inf.	"	9-19-14	
Hildrith, John P.	"	25th Inf.	"	1-1-14	
Hill, Caleb	Capt.Com.	McDonough's Fleet	Killed	8-16-14	
Hill, David	Private	23rd Inf.	Died	6-1-13	
Hill, George		Essex	Killed	3-28-14	
Hill, Hiram	Corporal	23rd Inf.	Died	2-28-14	
Hill, Hubbard D.		11th Inf.	"	2-10-13	
Hill, John	Private	22nd Inf.	"	5-22-14	
Hill, Lyman	"	5th Inf.	"	4-3-14	
Hill, Mark	Sailor	Essex	Killed	3-28-14	
Hill, William	Private	11th Inf.	Died	9-2-14	
Hillegas, John	"	4th Rfls.	"	8-20-14	
Hinckley, Samuel	"	45th Inf.	"	10-8-14	
Hindman, Robert	"	Ky. Mil.	"	10-30-12	
Hinds, William	"	2nd Art.	"	6-25-13	
Hines, Joseph	"	14th Inf.	"	4-5-14	
Hinhart, Abraham	Seaman	Globe	"	11-1-13	
Hinkley, Samuel	Private	45th Inf.	"	10-8-14	
Hinton, Rezin	"	28th Inf.	"	8-22-14	
Hiram, Arnold	"	4th Inf.	"	12-14-14	
Hobart,	Lieut.		Killed		at Ft. George
Hobart, Henry A.	1 Lieut.		"	5-27-13	
Hobbs,	Private	8th Inf.	Died	June 1814	
Hobbs, Abraham	"	10th Inf.	"	2-24-14	
Hobden, Francis		Va.	"	2-24-15	Dartmoor Prison
Hobson, John		N.C.	"	3-14-15	Dartmoor Prison
Hodgkins, John	Private	4th Inf.	"	2-4-14	
Hodgdon, Richard	"	9th Inf.	"	9-17-14	
Hoffman, John	Seaman	Lawrence	Killed	12-31-13	
Hoffner, Thomas	Private	Art.	Died	12-3-14	
Hogaboom, John	"	21st Inf.	"	1814	
Hogal, Barnabas	"	2nd Drag.	"	8-6-13	
Hogan, John	"	Ky. Mil.	"	1-9-15	
Hoit, Zebezee	"	4th Inf.	Killed	11-11-13	
Holbrook, Abijiah		Mass.	Died	3-10-15	Dartmoor Prison
Holcomb, Charles C.	Private	11th Inf.	"	12-10-12	
Holden, Francis		Va.	"	2-24-15	Dartmoor Prison
Holden, Henry		Mass.	"	4-6-15	Dartmoor Prison
Holder, Jesse	Private	18th Inf.	"	1-21-14	
Hollida, Edwin	"	8th Inf.	"	Nov. 1813	
Holland, Chas.	"	4th Inf.	"	12-14-14	

Name	Rank	Unit	Status	Date	Note
Holmes, Andrew H.	Major	32nd Inf.	Killed	8-4-14	
Holmes, David	Private	11th Inf.	Died	5-6-13	
Holmes, James, Jr.	"	21st Inf.	"	7-23-13	
Holmes, John	"	9th Inf.	"	8-20-14	
Holmes, John	"	11th Inf.	"	5-2-13	
Holmes, John	"	11th Inf.	"	Mar. 1814	
Holt, Jacob	Sailor	Mass	"	4-17-14	Chatham
Homan, William	Private	16th Inf.	"	7-18-13	
Hoofcot, John	Corporal	13th Inf.	"	7-22-13	
Hook, Greenbury	Sgt.	21st Inf.	"	10-15-14	
Hooker, Oris	Private	--	"	9-9-13	Quebec Prison
Hooper,	Captain	--	Killed	7-25-14	
Hooper,	Captain	N.Y. Vols.	"	11-11-13	
Hooper, Bryant	Private	16th Inf.	Died	12-11-13	
Hooper, Simon	"	--	"	7-28-13	Quebec Prison
Hoover, George	"	O.	"	1815	
Hopewell, Pollard	Sailor	Chesapeake	Killed	6-1-13	
Hopkins, Isom	Private	17th Inf	Died	7-15-15	
Hopkins, John	"	14th Inf.	"	8-15-13	
Hopkins, Joseph	"	O. Mil.	"	1812	
Hopkins, Joseph		--	Killed		at Ft.Meigs Seige
Hopkins, Philip	Private	14th Inf.	Died	Aug. 1813	
Hopper, John G.	"	Ky. Mil.	"	9-28-13	
Hoppock, John L.	Captain	15th Inf.	Killed	4-27-13	
Hord, Thomas	Private	Ky. Mil.	Died	10-4-13	
Horn, Daniel	"	9th Inf.	"	1-12-14	
Horton, Luman H.B.	"	9th Inf.	Killed	11-11-13	
Horton, Stephen	"	16th Inf.	Died	8-20-13	
Hotchkiss, J. T.	"	23rd Inf.	"	5-10-13	
Hotchkiss, John T		--	Killed	1812	at Queenstown
Hotchkiss, Silas		25th Inf.	Died	4-5-14	
Hough, Zachari	Private	Art.	"	--	
Houghtaling, David	Private	23rd Inf.	"	4-9-15	
Houk, Peter	"	23rd Inf.	"	7-16-13	
How, Joshua	"	Lt. Art.	"	7-27-13	
Howard, Caleb	"	3rd Art.	"	11-14-12	
Howard, Jona	"	25th Reg.	"	11-7-14	
Howard, Joseph	"	--	"	7-3-13	Quebec Prison
Howard, Ralph	"	4th Rfls.	"	--	
Howe, Samuel	"	3rd Art.	"	9-20-13	
Howell,	Lt.Sailor	President	Killed	1-5-14	
Howell, Joseph	Private	Lt. Drag.	Died	7-23-13	
Howlton, John	"	25th Inf.	"	9-19-14	
Hoyle, Frans M.	"	27th Inf.	"	1-6-15	
Hoyt, David H.	"	3rd Art.	"	--	
Hubbard, Christopher	Sailor	Md.	"	May 1814	Chatham
Hubbard, George	"	--	"	12-27-14	Chatham
Hubbard, Herbert	Private	35th Inf.	"	1-15-15	
Hubbard, Joseph I.	"	16th Inf.	"	5-17-14	
Hubbard, Roswell	"	3rd Art.	"	9-17-12	
Huber, John	"	15th Inf.	"	--	
Huckerson, Rice	"	8th Inf.	"	9-24-14	
Hudgins, W. D.	"	8th Inf.	"	12-4-13	
Hudson, Elisha	Sgt.	33rd Inf.	"	10-10-14	
Hudson, James	Private	12th Inf.	"	Feb. 1815	

Huff, Jonathan	Private	15th Inf.	Died	May 1813	
Hughes, Richa		N.Y.	"	2-5-14	Dartmoor Prison
Hughes, Richard		N.Y.	"	1-29-14	Dartmoor Prison
Hurlburt, Jehiel, Jr.	Private	O.Mil.3rd Reg.	"	Feb. 1813	
Hulbert, Silas	"	41st Inf.	"	Aug. 1814	
Hulbert, Simeon	"	6th Art.	"	Nov. 1813	
Hulett, Gold	"	10th Inf.	"	10-17-14	
Hull,	Captain	9th Inf.	Killed	11-11-13	
Hull, Abraham F.	"	9th Inf.	"	7-25-14	
Hull, Rouse	Private	25th Inf.	Died	8-17-13	
Hulse, John	"	N.J. Mil.	"	1815	
Hult, Foster	"	--	"	9-23-13	Quebec Prison
Hamilton, John	"	12th Inf.	"	7-21-14	
Humphrey, Saml.	"	1st Drag.	"	12-29-12	
Humphrey, W. L.	"	10th Inf.	"	6-24-13	
Hungate, John	"	5th Reg. Ky.Vols.Mil!	"	11-9-13	
Hunt,	Lieut.	--	Killed	7-25-14	
Hunt, Isaac	Private	Art.	Died	6-5-14	
Hunt, Isaac	"	11th Inf.	"	6-5-14	
Hunt, Solomon	"	--	"	8-4-13	Quebec Prison
Hunt, Thomas	Sgt.	9th Inf.	"	--	
Hunter,	Ensign	--	Killed	7-25-14	
Hunter,	"	25th Inf.	"	11-11-13	
Hunter, David	3 Lieut.	--	"	11-11-13	
Hunter, David		12th Inf.	"	11-11-13	
Hunter, James	Private	15th Inf.	Died	9-13-13	
Hunter, Joel	"	Art	"	--	
Hunter, William	"	2nd Art.	"	6-6-13	
Hunter, William C.	Ensign	25th Inf.	Killed	7-25-14	
Huntley, Lee	Private	13th Inf.	Died	9-2-15	
Hurst, Kemp W.	Sgt.	35th Inf.	"	2-9-15	
Hush, Samuel	Private	1st Rgt.	"	12-25-14	
Huskaby, John	"	21st Inf.	"	4-23-14	
Huskin, Noah	"	34th Inf.	"	11-25-13	
Huskins, Levi	"	25th Inf.	"	10-7-14	
Hussey, Zachariah	"	21st Inf.	"	9-7-13	
Husted, Joseph	"	4th Inf.	"	6-10-14	
Huston, James	"	Ky. Mil.	"	12-5-13	
Huston, William	Captain	O. Mil.	"	1812	
Hutchins,	Private	2nd Art.	"	7-16-13	
Hutchins, Emory	"	33rd Inf.	"	11-6-13	
Hutchins, William	"	2nd Art.	"	6-30-13	
Hutchinson, John	"	15th Inf.	"	4-15-14	
Hutchinson, Philip	"	21st Inf.	"	11-24-12	
Hutchinson, Rufus	"	31st Inf.	"	10-31-14	
Hutchinson, Thomas	Sailor	--	"	6-25-14	Chatham
Huzey, Henry	Private	45th Inf.	"	10-16-14	
Hyde, Joshua	"	11th Inf.	"	9-19-13	
Hydra, Dempey		N.C.	"	12-24-14	Dartmoor Prison

Ingalls, Jonathan	Private	--	Died	8-14-13	Quebec Prison
Ingersoll, Geo.	"	11th Inf.	"	4-13-13	
Ingram, Valentine	"	20th Inf.	"	Jan. 1814	
Ireland, Hezehiah	"	32nd Inf.	"	7-27-14	
Irvine, Christopher	Captain	--	Killed	5-5-13	
Irwin, John		--	"	1-22-13	
Ishum, Wm.	Seaman	Allegator	Died	7-1-14	
Israel, Francis	Private	6th Inf.	"	9-24-14	
Jacob, Lew		N.Y.	Died	12-7-14	Dartmoor Prison
Jacobs, Gilsic	Private	Ky. Mil.	"	9-17-13	
Jacoby, Peter	"	Pa. Mil. 8th Co.	"	9-7-14	
Jack,	Captain	1st Reg.Miss.Vols.	Killed	8-30-13	
Jackson, George	Private	12th Inf.	Died	--	
Jackson, Hezekiah	3 Lieut.	24th Inf.	"	8-4-14	
Jackson, John		Md.	"	3-14-15	Dartmoor Prison
Jackson, John		Essex	Killed	3-28-14	
Jackson, John	Seaman	Surprise	Drowned	4-5-15	
Jackson, A. H.	Private	21st Inf.	Died	9-26-14	
Jackson, Joseph		--	Killed	4-6-15	Dartmoor Prison
Jackson, Levi		US Inf.	Died	11-12-14	
Jackson, Noble	Private	6th Ky. Mil.	"	1-2-13	
Jackson, Robert	"	1st Rifles	"	6-12-15	
Jackson, Sam'l.	"	21st Inf.	"	7-2-13	
Jackson, Thomas		N.Y.	"	6-6-14	Dartmoor Prison
Jackson, Thomas		N.Y.	"	4-6-15	Dartmoor Prison
Jackson, Thomas		N.Y.	"	6-5-13	Dartmoor Prison
Jackson, William	Private	Ky. Mil.	"	10-19-13	
James, Alexander	Sgt.	Ky. Mil.	"	1-13-15	
James, Edgar		--	"	6-8-14	
James, Henry	13th	N.Y. Mil.	"	2-1-14	
James, Jacob	Private	12th Inf.	"	3-13-14	
James, John	"	21st Inf.	"	1-7-14	
James, Jourdan	"	7th US Inf.	"	5-15-14	
Jarvis, James		Mass.	"	1-24-14	Dartmoor Prison
Jenkins, Edw.		Mass.	"	2-24-15	
Jenkins, Jeremiah	Private	8th Inf.	"	11-10-14	
Jenkins, John		Gay Head	"	2-24-14	
Jenkins, Solomon	Seaman	Surprise	Drowned	4-5-15	
Jennings, John		--	Died	2-22-15	
Jennings, William		Essex	Killed	3-28-14	
Jennis, George	Private	11th Inf.	Died	3-23-13	

Jervice, Thomas		Mass.	Died	1-24-14	Dartmoor Prison
Jervil, David	Private	11th Inf.	"	2-17-13	
Jewett, John	"	US Inf.	"	1-28-14	
Jipson, Ruben	"	Art.	"	1-12-13	
John, Johannas		Mass.	"	1-8-15	Dartmoor Prison
John, Benjamin	Sgt.	O.	"	1814	
John, Jno	Private	17th Inf.	"	3-25-15	
Johnson, Alexander		S.C.	"	11-2-14	Dartmoor Prison
Johnson, David	Private	15th Inf.	"	4-7-14	
Johnson, Ebenezer	Seaman	Saratoga	Killed	9-11-14	
Johnson, Elisha		S.C.	Died	11-2-13	Dartmoor Prison
Johnson, Henry	Seaman	Ticonderoga	Killed	9-11-14	
Johnson, Isaac	Private	29th Inf.	Died	3-5-14	
Johnson, Isaac	"	21st Inf.	"	6-6-13	
Johnson, Jno		N.Y.	"	2-1-14	Dartmoor Prison
Johnson, Jno	Private	--	"	8-22-13	Dartmoor Prison
Johnson, John		N.Y.	"	2-1-15	Dartmoor Prison
Johnson, John	Private	22nd Inf.	"	1-10-15	
Johnson, John	Seaman	Surprise	Drowned	4-5-15	
Johnson, John	Sailor	N.Y.	Died	5-16-14	Chatham
Johnson, John	Private	Ky. Mil.	"	5-2-13	
Johnson, John		N.Y. Criterion	"	1814	Dartmoor Prison
Johnson, John K.	Corporal	Ky. Mil.	"	11-8-13	
Johnson, Joseph	Private	20th Inf.	"	3-15-14	
Johnson, Joseph T.	Seaman	--	Killed	4-6-15	Dartmoor Prison
Johnson, Lambert		N.J.	Died	6-25-14	Dartmoor Prison
Johnson, Lambert	Seaman	N.Y.	"	1813	
Johnson, Peter	"	Saratoga	Killed	9-11-14	
Johnson, Peter		Essex	"	3-28-14	
Johnson, S	O.S.	Alligator	Died	7-1-14	
Johnson, Sampson	Private	13th Inf.	"	7-8-13	
Johnson, Thomas	"	3rd Art.	"	11-23-12	
Johnson, Thomas	"	4th Inf.	"	11-25-14	
Johnson, Thomas	"	41st Inf.	"	1-10-15	
Johnson, T. T.	Mate	Alligator	"	4-1-14	
Johnson, Wm.		Mass.	"	3-10-15	Dartmoor Prison
Johnson, Wm.	Private	9th Inf.	"	9-12-14	
Johnson, William		Essex	Killed	3-28-14	
Johnson, William	Private	25th Inf.	Died	5-31-13	
Johnson, William	"	7th US Inf.	"	3-30-14	
Johnston, Eben		Champ. Squad	Killed	9-11-14	
Johnston, Peter	Private	7th U.S. Inf.	Died	4-19-14	
Jonas, Hugh	"	41st Inf.	"	5-28-14	
Jones,	Sgt.	1st Reg.US Art.	Killed	10-30-13	
Jones, Abraham	Private	7th US Inf.	Died	5-25-14	
Jones, Almiran	"	131st Inf.	"	4-27-13	
Jones, Amos	"	12th Inf.	"	--	
Jones, Enoch B.	"	16th Inf.	"	4-24-14	
Jones, George		Conn.	"	4-30-14	Dartmoor Prison
Jones, Jacob		Md.	"	2-23-15	Dartmoor Prison
Jones, James	Private	16th Inf.	"	11-23-13	
Jones, James	Seaman	Lawrence	"	12-31-13	
Jones, James		Md.	"	2-23-15	Dartmoor Prison
Jones, John		President-St.Thomas	"	1814	Dartmoor Prison
Jones, John	Private	16th Inf.	"	12-8-12	

Jones, John	Private	13th Inf.	Died	9-15-14	
Jones, John	"	10th Inf.	"	11-7-14	
Jones, John		St. Thomas	"	2-8-15	Dartmoor Prison
Jones, Moses	Private	23rd Inf.	"	8-28-13	
Jones, Joshua		12th Reg.Va.Inf.	"	Nov. 1813	
Jones, Joshua	Seaman	US Argus	Killed	8-14-13	
Jones, Julius	Private	6th Ky. Mil.	Died	10-4-12	
Jones, Peter	Major	Va. Mil.	"	1815	
Jones, Richard	Private	US Inf.	"	3-14-14	
Jones, Samuel	"	15th Inf.	"	3-3-14	
Jones, Saml.	"	15th Inf.	"	3-15-14	
Jones, Samuel	Sailor	N.Y.	"	2-5-14	
Jones, Simeon	Corporal	9th Inf	"	--	
Jones, Thomas		--	"	6-6-13	Dartmoor Prison
Jones, William		Mass.	"	11-4-14	Dartmoor Prison
Jordan, Jeremiah	Private	12th Inf.	"	--	
Jordan, Joseph	Mate	Argus	Killed	8-14-13	
Jordan, Robert	Private	38th Inf.	Died	2-22-15	
Jordon, Miles	"	3rd Rfls.	"	2-18-15	
Jordon, William	"	36th Inf.	"	1-14-15	
Joseph, Emanuel		--	"	11-25-14	Dartmoor Prison
Joseph, George	Sgt.	Ky. Mil.	"	5-5-13	
Joseph, Peter		Fr. W.I.	"	2-26-15	Dartmoor Prison
Judd, Wm.	Private	--	"	11-7-13	Quebec Prison
Justice, Thomas		Lawrence	"	9-10-13	
Kean, Henry	Private	16th Inf.	Died	12-31-14	
Keeler, Isaac	"	9th Inf.	"	1-30-15	
Keeling, John C.		Essex	Killed	3-28-14	
Keen, Daniel	Private	15th Inf.	Died	1-9-15	
Keen, Hervey R.	"	1st Rfls.	"	--	
Keeney, James	"	7th Inf.	"	2-20-14	
Keesecker, Conrad	"	5th Reg.Va.Mil.	"	5-2-13	
Kehr, John D.	1 Lieut.	22nd Inf.	Killed	7-25-14	
Keilholtz, William	Corporal	1st Balto.Vol.Art.	Died	1-21-15	
Keimback, Adam	Private	15th Inf.	"	9-2-13	
Keith, Arel	"	14th Inf.	"	4-20-14	
Kelley, Abraham	"	26th Inf.	"	2-23-14	
Kelley, James	"	Com. Mil.	"	1813	
Kelly, George	"	6th Inf.	"	1-22-13	
Kelly, John		Mass.	"	2-26-15	Dartmoor Prison
Kelly, John C.	Private	Lawrence	Killed	12-31-13	
Kelly, Joseph	"	4th Inf.	Died	Jan. 1814	

Name	Rank	Unit	Fate	Date	Notes
Kelly, Michael	Private	2nd Art.	Died	6-6-13	
Kelly, Michael	Q.M.	Chesapeake	Killed	6-1-13	
Kelly, Morgan	Private	14th N.Y. Vols	Died	8-30-14	
Kelly, William	"	4th Inf.	"	6-16-14	
Kelton, Ebenezer	"	25th Inf.	"	11-30-13	
Kelton, James	"	4th Inf.	"	11-16-14	
Kemble, Jacob		--	"	4-16-15	Dartmoor Prison
Kenedy, Joseph	Seaman	Lawrence	"	12-31-13	
Kennada, Robert	Private	34th Inf.	"	11-28-13	
Kennady, Henry		Essex	Killed	5-4-14	
Kennady, Henry	Mate	Essex	"	3-28-14	
Kennedy, Henry	Mate	Essex	"	7-3-14	
Kennedy, Thomas	Private	1st Rfls.	Died	10-11-14	
Kennel, Casper	"	Ky. Inf.	"	12-21-14	
Kent, Benjamin	"	15th Inf.	"	3-12-14	
Kerr, Nathaniel Preston		O. Mil.	"	3-31-13	
Kertly, Lewis	Private	3rd Ky. Mil.	"	12-10-12	
Kesler, Henry	"	1st Rfl.	"	8-16-13	
Kesterson, Thomas W.	"	24th Inf.	"	8-4-14	
Ketrope, James		Mass.	"	11-11-14	Dartmoor Prison
Keyley, Henry	Private	22nd Inf.	"	7-25-14	
Kilbough, Frederick	Lieut.	Pa. Mil.	"	9-9-13	
Kilday, Henry	Private	24th Inf.	"	12-19-13	
Kilgore, William	Captain	O. Mil.	"	1814	
Kilham, John	Private	23rd Inf.	"	11-7-12	
Kilton, James	"	4th Inf.	"	11-16-14	
Kimball, Abel	Lieut.	Drag.	"	2-10-15	
Kimball, Benjs	Private	--	"	8-5-13	Quebec Prison
Kimball, Stephen	"	37th Inf	"	10-25-14	
Kimball, Timothy	"	45th Inf.	"	10-31-14	
Kincaid, James	"	1st Inf.	"	11-4-14	
King, Adam	"	16th Inf.	"	6-5-14	
King, Alexander	"	15th Inf.	"	12-20-12	
King, George	Lieut.	Art.	"	--	
King, Uriah		Mass	"	2-3-15	Dartmoor Prison
Kingsbury, Eleazer	Private	19th Inf.	"	7-18-13	
Kingsland, Christopher	"	6th Inf.	"	3-6-14	
Kinkaid, John	"	1st Inf.	"	11-4-14	
Kinney, Benj.	"	4th Rfl.	"	8-9-14	
Kinney, Joseph	Captain	Inf.	Killed	7-25-14	
Kinney, William	Private	2nd Reg.Tenn.Vols.	Died	1815	Serving in Fla.
Kithcart, Joseph	"	O. Mil.	"	2-24-14	
Knapp, James		--	"	2-27-15	Dartmoor Prison
Knapps, James		Md.	"	2-26-15	Dartmoor Prison
Knight, Andw.	Private	--	"	8-27-13	Quebec Prison
Knight, Paul	"	4th Inf.	"	1-6-14	
Knight, Joshua	"	14th Inf.	"	6-12-13	
Knowlton, Joshua	"	23rd Inf.	"	--	
Knowlton, Wm.	Seaman	Argus	Killed	8-14-13	
Knott, Jeremiah	Private	Ky. Mil.	Died	1-15-15	
Koons, Daniel	"	2nd Pa. Mil.	"	11-15-15	
Koster, Joel	"	31st Inf.	"	9-18-14	
Kruson, Jacob	"	16th Inf.	"	11-11-14	
Kyle, Samuel	"	1st Rfls.	"	1814	

Name	Rank	Unit	Status	Date	Notes
Lackey, Amosa	Private	--	Died	4-2-13	Quebec Prison
Lain, Benj.	"	--	"	7-23-13	Quebec Prison
Lainhard, David	"	11th Inf.	"	8-25-14	
Lamb,	Midshipman	Lawrence	Killed	9-10-13	
Lamb, Abner	Private	5th Inf.	Died	12-4-13	
Lamb, Anthony,	Com.	--	"	11-22-14	Dartmoor Prison
Lamb, David	Corp.	2nd Reg.Mass.Mil.	"	4-18-15	
Lamb, Josiah P.	Private	--	"	2-12-13	Quebec Prison
Lambert,	Captain	--	"	4-10-13	(about)
Lambert, Samuel	Private	27th Inf.	"	12-6-14	
Lamson, Charles		Md.	"	1-15-14	Dartmoor Prison
Lamphier, John	Private	11th Inf.	"	9-13-14	
Lancaster, Willm	"	21st Inf.	"	1-15-15	
Lander, Charles	"	21st Inf.	"	7-11-13	
Lander, Chas.	"	--	"	7-22-13	Quebec Prison
Landon, John	"	25th Inf.	"	--	
Lane, Dennis	"	34th Inf.	Killed	10-1-13	
Lane, Samuel	"	Co.2 Pa. Mil.	Died	2-18-14	
Langley, Thomas	"	21st Inf.	"	8-20-14	
Langley, Thomas	"	7th Inf.	"	11-30-14	
Lansdown, William	"	20th Inf.	"	3-11-15	
Lanton, Perry	"	--	"	7-20-13	Quebec Prison
Lapsley, William	"	Art.	"	6-9-13	
Laraway, Jacob	Seaman	Saratoga	Killed	9-11-14	
Lark, John	Private	7th US Inf.	Died	5-27-14	
Larkin, Lewis		N.H.	"	9-30-14	Dartmoor Prison
Larkins, Amos		Mass.	"	1-27-14	Dartmoor Prison
Larkins, Lewis		"	"	9-30-13	Dartmoor Prison
Larney, Cornelius	Private	15th Inf.	"	2-27-13	
Larrabee,	Lieut.	--	Killed		at Odell Town
Lamb, Henry	Midshipman	Lawrence	"	12-31-13	
Lamb, Henry	"	US Squadron	"	9-10-13	
Landerdale, James	Lt.Col.	--	"	12-23-14	
Laskey, James		Mass.	Died	2-4-15	Dartmoor Prison
Lasol, Jesse		Martineque	"	11-3-14	Dartmoor Prison
Latham, Dudley	Private	25th Inf.	"	6-26-13	
Lawrence, Benj.	Corporal	23rd Inf.	"	--	
Lawrence, Isaac	Private	13th Inf.	"	--	
Lawrence, James	"	3rd Art.	"	10-15-13	
Lawrence, James	Captain	Chesapeake	"	6-1-13	mortally wounded
Lawrence, John		Champ. Squad	Killed	9-11-14	
Lawrence, Thomas	Private	Art.	Died	--	
Lawton, Perry	"	9th Inf.	"	7-20-13	
Layor, John	"	17th Inf.	"	3-1-15	
Leach, James	"	21st Reg. Inf.	Killed	7-25-14	Battle of Niagara
Leapatch, John Ann		Mass.	Died	1815	
Leathers, Stephen	Private	30th Inf.	"	4-15-15	

Leavenworth, Lemuel	Private	25th Inf.	Died	Dec. 1813	
LeBaron, James	"	9th Inf.	"	12-18-13	
Lebor, Jacob	"	6th Inf.	"	6-16-14	
Lebourveau, Denas	"	11th Inf.	"	5-6-14	
Lee, Charles	"	16th Inf.	"	12-25-12	
Lee, Daniel	"	11th Inf.	"	9-7-14	
Lee, David M.	"	11th Inf.	"	8-14-14	
Lee, George	"	40th Inf.	"	4-3-15	
Lee, Richard		Mass.	"	12-30-14	Dartmoor Prison
Lee, William		Essex	Killed	3-28-14	
Leech, Samuel	Private	38th Inf.	Died	--	
Leeds, James	"	3rd Art.	"	1-6-14	
Legan, Miller W.	Sgt.	8th Inf.	"	8-1-13	
Legate, Elijah	Private	6th Ky. Mil.	"	11-22-12	
Legg, Stephen	"	9th Inf.	"	10-8-13	
Lemane, James	"	14th Inf.	"	10-15-14	
Leming, Benjamin	"	17th Inf.	"	1-12-14	
Lemmon, Benj.	"	17th Inf.	"	12-27-14	
Lendman, Francis	"	11th Inf.	"	12-25-14	
Leonard, George	"	34th Inf.	"	10-20-13	
Leopatch, Jno.		Mass	"	2-9-14	Dartmoor Prison
Lepiate,	Capt.	N.Y.	"	3-10-15	Dartmoor Prison
Lerch, Peter, Sr.	Private	Pa. Mil.	"	2-24-13	
Lesiville, Thomas	"	25th Inf.	"	11-16-14	
Lesley, Samuel	Sgt.	Lt. Art.	"	--	
Lester, Bennet	Private	27th Inf.	"	12-29-14	
Lester, Jason		Md.	"	1-1-13	Dartmoor Prison
Lestor, James		--	"	1-1-14	Dartmoor Prison
Letcher, Henry		N.Y.	"	1-24-13	
Leverett, William		N.Y.	"	4-6-15	Dartmoor Prison
Leveridge, William		--	Killed	4-6-15	Dartmoor Prison
Levers, John		14th Inf.	Died	2-9-15	
Levett, Joseph	Private	9th Inf.	"	--	
Levi, Henry	"	23rd Inf.	"	--	
Levins, Wm.	"	15th Inf.	"	--	
Levitt, Thomas	"	45th Inf.	"	2-8-15	
Lewary, Joseph	"	15th Inf.	"	9-9-13	
Lewis,		Art.	Killed	10-30-12	
Lewis, Armistead G.A.	Capt.	Rifles	"	9-17-14	
Lewis, Doughty	Private	15th Inf.	Died	Dec. 1814	
Lewis, James	Sailor	N.Y.	"	1-7-14	Chatham
Lewis, Jno.		R.I.	"	8-5-13	Dartmoor Prison
Lewis, Jno.	Private	--	"	9-1-13	Quebec Prison
Lewis, John		R.I.	"	8-5-14	Dartmoor Prison
Lewis, John	Private	7th US Inf.	"	5-28-14	
Lewis, John	"	1st Art.	"	3-2-14	
Lewis, Joseph	"	15th Inf.	"	5-13-14	
Lewis, Lewis	"	6th Inf.	"	5-24-14	
Lewis, Thomas (boy)		Brig. Eagle	Killed	9-11-14	
Lewis, Thomas	Capt.	--	"	5-5-13	
Lewis, Thomas G.	Private	23rd Inf.	Died	5-13-14	
Libbey, Thomas	"	--	"	2-25-13	Quebec Prison
Libby, Amos	"	34th Inf.	Killed	10-26-13	
Libby, Humphrey	"	3rd Art.	Died	10-18-13	
Liggett, James	Ensign	17th Inf.	Killed	9-25-12	

Name	Rank	Unit	Fate	Date	Location
Light, Wm.	Sailor	--	Died	3-12-14	Chatham
Lillie, Rufus I.	Private	11th Inf.	"	7-5-14	
Lindman, Jacob	Seaman	Eagle	"	9-11-14	
Lindsley, David	Private	11th Inf.	"	12-22-13	
Lindsley, Jonathan	"	42nd Inf.	"	--	
Linsey, John	"	34th Inf.	"	9-28-14	
Lint, Lewis	"	Dragoons	"	1-13-15	
Liscum, Peleliah D.	Sgt.	21st Inf.	"	7-1-13	
Lister, Jacob	Private	16th Inf.	"	--	
Liswell, Thomas	"	25th US Inf.	"	11-16-14	
Lisweller, Thos.	"	25th US Inf.	"	9-19-14	
Litteral, John	"	19th Inf.	"	5-15-13	
Littlefield, Geo.	"	21st Inf.	"	2-14-15	
Littlefield, Joseph	"	9th Inf.	"	12-25-13	
Littleton, Pursley	"	Art.	"	1-4-15	
Livers, John	"	14th Inf.	"	--	
Livingston, Courtland	Midshipman		Killed	6-1-13	
Lloyd, David	Private	13th Inf.	Died	8-17-13	
Lloyd, James	General	--	"	1815	in Md.
Locker, John A.	Private	23rd Inf.	"	5-14-15	
Locy, Ezra	"	3rd Art.	"	June 1814	
Lodowich, Morson	Major	--	Killed	8-4-14	
Logan, Robert	Lt.	17th US Inf.	"	1-22-13	River Raisin
Logue, Joseph	Private	22nd Inf.	Died	11-19-12	
Long, George	"	1st Inf.	"	12-21-14	
Long, Moses	"	--	"	10-15-14	
Longacre, Daniel	"	Pa. Mil.	"	1812	
Longstreet, Dan'l.	"	15th Inf.	"	9-8-13	
Loomis, Milton	"	25th Inf.	"	11-11-13	
Loper, John	"	135th Reg. Pa.Mil.	"	1812	In Camp
Lord, Jacob	"	9th Inf.	"	12-27-13	
Lorly, Placid		Wash.	"	11-1-14	Dartmoor Prison
Loshley, Call	Private	8th Inf.	"	9-13-14	
Lossole,	"	22nd Inf.	"	9-19-14	
Loud, Warren	"	9th Inf.	"	11-16-14	
Louvre, Jno.	"	22nd Inf.	"	9-19-14	
Love, David	"	12th Inf.	"	--	
Lovejoy, Wm. O.	"	11th Inf.	"	10-25-13	
Lovel, Joseph	"	Fr. W.I.	"	11-3-14	Dartmoor Prison
Loveland, Chester C.	Lt.	Art.	"	3-28-13	
Lovely,	Pr.	N.C.	"	11-1-14	Dartmoor Prison
Lovely,	Dr.	Hawk-Wash.,D.C.	"	1815	Dartmoor Prison
Low, John	Private	11th Inf.	"	3-26-13	
Lowe, John M.	1 Lt.	N.Y. Mil.	Killed	12-19-13	At Niagara
Lozier, Nicholas	Private	2nd Drags.	Died	11-1-13	
Lozier, Nicholas	"	Drag.	"	10-24-13	
Luce, William	"	9th Inf.	"	6-28-13	
Ludlow, Augustus C.	Lt.	Chesapeake	"	--	
Ludlow, James	Sailor	Conn.	"	3-30-14	Chatham
Ludlow, Reuben	"	N.Y.	"	2-23-14	Chatham
Ludwell, Lee	Private	17th Inf.	"	7-22-13	
Lufkey, Jas.		Mass.	"	2-4-14	Dartmoor Prison
Lufkey, James		Enterprize-Mass	"	1813	Dartmoor Prison
Lumes, Joel	Private	Lt. Drag.	Killed	9-12-14	

Lusk, Amos	Capt.	O.	Died	5-13-13	
Lustin, Richard		U.S. Inf.	"	11-1-14	
Lyman, Hill	Private	5th Inf.	"	4-3-14	
Lyman, Leonard		11th Inf.	"	1-5-13	
Lyndsay, William		5th Inf.	Killed	June 1813	
Lynch, John	1 Lt.	14th Inf.	"	11-11-13	
Lynds, David	Private	25th Inf.	Died	12-1-12	
Lyon, Thomas	Capt.	16th Inf.	Killed	4-27-13	
Lyster, Wm.	Private	10th Inf.	Died	6-26-13	

MacDonald	Ensign	1st Reg. Miss. Vols.	Killed	8-30-13	
Mack, David	Private	14th Inf.	Died	11-29-14	
Mackley, Aaron	Sailor	Conn.	"	4-1-14	Chatham
Mackubin, Richard Creagh	Private	22nd Art. Reg.	"	8-24-14	
Macky, John		Md.	"	11-18-14	Dartmoor Prison
Macres, Samuel		11th Inf.	"	Apr. 1814	
Macumber, James	Cpl.	33rd Inf.	"	--	
Madosa, Calasso		--	"	10-27-14	Dartmoor Prison
Maloney, James	Private	16th Inf.	"	1-1-14	
Maloney, Thomas	Seaman	Saratoga	Killed	9-11-14	
Malter, D.	Private	38th Inf.	Died	2-25-14	
Manahan, John	"	6th Ky. Mil.	"	12-24-12	
Manjoy, William	"	12th Inf.	"	4-10-14	
Manley, Ray	"	12th Inf.	"	10-29-14	
Mann, Asa	"	29th Inf.	"	10-6-14	
Mann, Daniel	Sgt.	Lt. Art.	"	12-10-14	
Mann, Jabez		Mass.	"	4-6-15	Dartmoor Prison
Mann, James	Seaman		Killed	4-6-15	Dartmoor Prison
Mann, John	Private	2nd Art.	Died	3-22-14	
Mann, William	"	34th Inf.	"	11-13-14	
Manning, Nathl.	"	9th Inf.	"	9-16-14	
Mansee, Daniel	"	N.Y. Vols	"	8-23-14	
Mansfield, Fisher	Sailor	Conn.	"	4-1-14	Chatham
Mansfield, Saml.	Private	25th Inf.	"	9-27-14	
Manzey, John L.	"	20th Inf.	"	5-30-13	
Marcellus, Cornelius	"	25th Inf.	"	8-19-14	
March, Jesse		Me.	"	2-5-15	Dartmoor Prison
Marchant, Joseph	Private	O.	"	1813	
Marchens, Jesse		Me.	"	2-3-15	Dartmoor Prison
Marcy, Wm. P.	Private	11th Inf.	"	11-11-13	
Marino, Alex		Chesapeake	Killed	6-1-13	
Marley, William	Private	1st Rfls.	Died	6-20-14	
Marlow, Thomas	"	14th Inf.	"	1-15-15	

Marsh, Wm.	Private	17th Inf.	Died	1-13-14	
Marshall, Benjamin		Mass.	"	3-27-15	Dartmoor Prison
Marshall, Lewis	Private	Art.	"	5-30-14	
Marshall, Sola		Mass.	"	11-20-14	Dartmoor Prison
Marshall, Reuben		Essex	Killed	5-4-14	
Marshall, Reuben	Q.M.	Essex	"	7-3-14	
Marshall, Reuben	Gunner		"	3-28-14	
Marshall, Robert	Private	Ky.Vol.Mil.	Died	1814	
Marshall, Sol		Mass.	"	2-17-14	Dartmoor Prison
Marshall, William	Private	21st Inf.	"	9-29-14	
Martial, Geo.	"	22nd Inf.	"	10-17-14	
Martial, Saml.		Mass.	"	11-20-14	Dartmoor Prison
Martin, Daniel		Navy	Killed	10-6-12	
Martin, David	Private	11th Inf.	Died	9-25-14	
Martin, Daniel		La.	"	9-22-13	Dartmoor Prison
Martin, David	Private	11th Inf.	"	8-30-14	
Martin, Edward		Lawrence	Killed	9-10-13	
Martin, James		Wasp	"	10-18-12	
Martin, James	Sgt.	Ky. Drag.	Died	10-5-13	
Martin, John		Carthagena	"	12-17-14	Dartmoor Prison
Martin, Joseph	Boatswain	Wasp	Killed	9-1-14	
Martin, Manuel		N.Y.	Died	9-22-14	Dartmoor Prison
Martin, Silvanus	Private	--	"	8-3-13	Quebec Prison
Martin, Thomas	"	29th Inf.	"	9-29-14	
Martin, William	"	21st Inf.	"	6-21-13	
Martinburgh, J.	(boy)	Alligator	"	7-1-14	
Mason, Alexander		O. Mil. Vols	"	--	
Mason, Beniah	Private	34th Inf.	"	10-1-14	
Mason, Simson	"	Ky. Mil.	"	3-28-14	
Mass, Theodore	"	Ky. Mil.	"	6-9-13	
Massie, Nathaniel		O. Mil.	"	11-3-13	
Matheny, John	Private	10th Inf.	"	1-1-14	
Mathew, Guy		O. Mil.	Killed	8-16-12	
Mathews, John		34th Inf.	Died	11-13-13	
Matlock, Francis	Private	5th Inf.	"	1813	
Matson, John	"	16th Inf.	"	12-10-14	
Mattocks, Jacob	"	22nd Inf.	"	1-22-14	
Maurice, Peter L.	"	2nd Art.	"	June 1813	
Mawheter, Wm.	"	14th NY Vols&Pa.Vols	"	9-16-14	
Maxwell, Simeon	"	21st Inf.	"	10-6-13	
Maxwell, Stephen	"	11th Inf.	"	7-5-14	
Maxwell, Thos.	"	--	"	2-20-13	Quebec Prison
Maxwell, Willm. F.	"	1st Art.	"	4-1-13	
May, John	"	17th Inf.	"	12-24-14	
Mayfield, Zach		Essex	Killed	3-28-14	
Mayhew, Christian	Q.M.	Lawrence	"	9-10-13	
Mayhew, Christian		Lawrence	Died	12-31-13	
Mayo,	Private	8th Inf.	"	June 1814	
Mays, Jno.		17th Inf.	"	12-31-14	
Mays, Wilson	Mate	Lawrence	Killed	12-31-13	
McAllister, Archibald	Private	4th Inf.	Died	11-30-13	
McAmy, Saml.	"	17th Inf.	"	1-20-15	
McAnally, John	"	22nd Inf.	"	--	
McCarty, William	(Quaker - Aiding Needy)		"	1-21-13	
McCannon, John	Private	25th Inf.	"	--	

Name	Rank	Unit	Status	Date	Notes
McClanaghan	Lt.		Killed	5-5-13	
M'Clannahan, Elijah	Major	Constitution	"	--	
McClease, Cornelius	Private	23rd Inf.	Died	12-4-14	
McClellan, William	"	N. Vols	Killed	9-14-14	
McClelland, Enos	"	22nd Inf.	Died	2-22-14	
McClelland, Michael	Captain	7th Inf.	Killed	12-23-14	
McClung, John	"	27th Reg.Va.Mil.	Died	1815	
McColvin, John	Private	Art.	Died	12-19-14	
McComas, Harry Gough	"	Sharp Shooters	Killed	9-14-14	North Point, Md.
McComb, Jno.	"	17th Inf.	Died	6-17-15	
McConemy, John	"	7th Inf.	"	1-21-15	
McCord, Alex r	Corporal	28th Inf.	"	9-18-14	
McCoy, David	Private	25th Inf.	"	7-4-13	
McCoy, Neal		Ft. Harrison	Killed	9-4-12	
McCracken, Virgil	Captain	--	Killed	1-22-13	
McCrae, Mathew	Private	7th Inf.	Died	2-14-15	
McCrie, James	Surgeon	25th Reg.	"	1814	
McCrief, John	Private	2nd Art.	"	10-30-13	
McCrossen, James	"	Art.	"	7-25-14	
McCullock,	Captain	--	Killed	8-5-12	
McCune, Samuel	Ensign	Pa. Mil.	Died	11-16-13	
McCurdel, John	Private	21st Inf.	"	6-11-13	
McCurry, William	"	US Inf.	"	3-2-14	
McDaniel, Joseph	"	US Inf.	"	8-4-14	
McDonald, David	"	23rd Inf.	"	9-30-14	
McDonald, Elisha		6th Inf.	"	--	
McDonald, James	Private	12th Inf.	"	4-10-14	
McDonald, Randall	Seaman	Saratoga	Killed	9-11-14	
McDonald, Stephen	Private	17th Inf.	Died	1-10-15	
McDonald, Thomas	"	15th Inf.	"	8-24-13	
McDonogh, Patrick	1 Lt.	--	Killed	8-15-14	
M'Donovan, Rollen		Mass	Died	11-18-14	Dartmoor Prison
McDonough, Jas.	Private	1st Art.	"	12-19-12	
McDonough,	Lt.	--	Killed		Fort Erie
McDonough, Patrick	1 Lt.	Art,	"	8-15-14	
McDowell, Wm.	Private	2nd Art.	Died	2-15-13	
McElhany, Wm.	"	22nd Inf.	"	1-11-14	
McFall, George	"	7th US Inf.	"	3-3-14	
McFarland,	Major	23rd Inf.	Killed	11-11-13	
McFarland, Daniel	"	--	"	7-25-14	
McGahy, John	Private	6th Inf.	Died	12-3-13	
McGavock,	Captain	Tenn. Mil.	Killed	1-24-14	
McGee, James	Private	2nd Art.	Died	10-9-12	
McGill, William	Lieut.	Art.	"	7-22-13	
McGrath, John	Private	2nd Art.	"	12-27-12	
McHenry, James	Major	Pa. Mil.	"	1812	
McIntire, Timm	Private	9th Inf.	"	11-11-13	
McIntosh, Garret	"	5th Inf.	"	11-2-12	
McIntosh, James	"	13th Inf.	"	6-28-14	
McIntyre, Robert		13th Inf.	"	10-13-12	
McIntyre, Jas.		--	"	12-23-13	Quebec Prison
McIlvaine, Thos.		--	Killed	1-22-13	
McKaig, Hugh	Private	16th Inf.	Died	--	
McKee, William	"	11th Inf.	"	3-20-13	
McKenzie, Alexander	"	23rd Inf.	"	Aug. 1813	
McKervin, Charles	"	7th Inf.	"	2-24-15	

Name	Rank	Unit	Fate	Date	Prison
McKinley, Danl.	Private	16th Inf.	Died	--	
McKinney,	Captain	25th Inf.	Killed	11-11-13	
McKinney,	Private	26th Inf.	Died	8-30-14	
McKinzie, David	"	--	"	10-20-13	Quebec Prison
McLean, Allison	"	Ky. Mil.	"	2-15-15	
McLean, Charles	Lieut.	25th Inf.	"	4-28-13	
McLaughlin, John	Private	45th Inf.	"	10-18-14	
McLaughlin, Preston		Ky. Mil.	"	3-11-14	
McLorely, Jas.	Private	2nd Art.	"	2-4-14	
McMillen, Arch d	"	--	"	8-12-13	Quebec Prison
McMullen, Hugh	"	6th Inf.	"	--	
McMurphy, John	"	21st Inf.	"	1-12-14	
McMurtry, James	"	27th Inf.	"	8-31-14	
McNaly, John	"	6th Inf.	"	5-25-14	
McNay, Edw.	"	22nd Inf.	"	10-27-14	
McShrigley, John	"	23rd Inf.	"	1-21-14	
McStewart, John	"	9th Inf.	"	2-18-13	
Meachum, Benj.'n	"	3rd Art.	"	12-15-13	
Mead, James	Captain	--	Killed	1-22-13	
Meadford, Joseph	Private	5th Inf.	Died	8-15-13	
Meadows, Williams	"	12th Inf.	"	1-17-14	
Mealate, Archibald	"	34th Inf.	"	9-15-14	
Meason, Thomas	General	Pa. Mil.	"	3-10-13	
Medcalf, John D.	Private	42nd Inf.	"	--	
Medoza, Charles		Carthegina	"	10-27-14	Dartmoor Prison
Meech, Joshua	Private	25th Inf.	"	8-23-14	
Meed, James	Captain	17th Inf.	Killed	1-22-13	
Megroth, John	Private	33rd Inf.	Died	12-11-13	
Mellin, Jacob	"	1st Inf.	"	10-28-14	
Mellin, Joshua	"	Art.	"	3-24-15	
Melpatrick, Hector	"	16th Inf.	"	12-14-12	
Melvin, John	"	40th Inf.	"	6-11-14	
Menter, Charles	"	Portugal	"	2-27-14	Dartmoor Prison
Mercer, Nathl. B.	"	--	"	1-28-13	Quebec Prison
Meredith, Obed.	"	2nd Reg. O. Mil.	"	5-3-14	
Merrill, Eli	"	--	"	9-26-13	Quebec Prison
Merris, William	"	29th Inf.	"	8-22-14	
Merry, John		Md.	"	11-18-14	Dartmoor Prison
Merton, James	Private	45th Inf.	"	--	
Messenger, Charles	Gunner	Marines	"	9-13-14	
Messenger, Wm. S.	Private	11th Inf.	"	--	
Messervey, Solomon	"	45th Inf.	"	--	
Mesler, Richard		--	"	11-20-14	Dartmoor Prison
Mester, Richard		Snap Dragon	"	1814	Dartmoor Prison
Meyers, Geo.	Private	14th N.Y. Vol.	"	9-13-14	
Michael, Andrew	Seaman	Lawrence	Killed	12-31-13	
Middleton,	Captain	1st Reg. Miss. Vols.	"	8-30-13	
Middleton, John	Sgt.	10th Inf.	Died	12-22-13	
Midge, Joseph		--	"	1-30-14	Dartmoor Prison
Miers, Charlton	Private	10th Inf.	"	12-2-13	
Miles, John	"	42nd Inf.	"	--	
Miles, Scills	"	35th Inf.	"	12-14-14	
Miles, Thomas	"	5th Inf.	"	7-5-14	
Mill, La Colle		--	Killed		Fort Strother
Miller, Ashville	Private	25th Inf.	Died	10-5-14	
Miller, Ashbill	"	25th Inf.	"	8-30-14	

Name	Rank	Unit	Status	Date	Place
Miller, Edward	Private	N.J.	Died	2-21-15	Dartmoor Prison
Miller, Edward		Monmouth,N.Y.	"	1813	Dartmoor Prison
Miller, Clement Harvey	Surgeon	1st Rfls.Ky.Mil.	Killed	1-23-13	River Raisin
Miller, Ezekiel	Sailor	N.Y.	Died	3-22-14	Chatham
Miller, Francis	Private	4th Rifles	"	--	
Miller, Frederick	"	Ky. Mil.	"	1-3-15	
Miller, Henry	"	16th US Inf.	"	7-24-13	
Miller, Josiah	"	23rd Inf.	"	1813	
Miller, Leonard	"	2nd Lt. Drag.	"	3-15-14	
Miller, Matthew	Corporal	2nd Reg.Tenn.Vols.	"	12-9-13	
Miller, Richard		Pa.	"	11-20-14	Dartmoor Prison
Miller, Robert	Private	22nd Inf.	"	2-3-14	
Miller, Robert	"	11th Inf.	"	--	
Miller, Samuel	Sailor	N.Y.	"	3-29-14	Chatham
Millery, Henry	Private	Ky. Inf.	"	11-1-14	
Mills,	Col.	--	Killed	5-29-13	Sachets Harbor
Mills, Adam L.	Sgt.	Ky. Drag.	Died	10-5-13	
Mills, Amos S.	Private	5th Inf.	"	7-25-14	
Mills, Chas.	"	--	"	12-16-13	
Mills, James	Sailor	Va.	"	6-10-14	Chatham
Mills, Jno.	Lt. Col.	--	Killed	5-29-13	
Mills, John	Private	20th Inf.	Died	--	
Mills, Jonathan	"	11th Inf.	"	3-2-15	
Mills, Williams		N.J.	"	3-24-15	Dartmoor Prison
Mims, Samuel	Lieut.	--	"	8-30-13	Fort Mims
Miner, Walker	Private	9th Inf.	"	12-13-14	
Mingo, Albert		La.	"	10-25-14	Dartmoor Prison
Mingus, Daniel		O. Vol. Mil.	Killed	11-30-12	
Minor, William	Corporal	Ky. Mil.	Died	10-28-13	
Minton, Nathan	Private	N.J. Mil.	"	2-8-13	
Minton, Nathaniel	"	15th Inf.	"	--	
Miston, Wm.		Md.	"	2-14-15	Dartmoor Prison
Mitchel, John	Seaman	N.Y.	"	June 1814	Stapleton Prison
Mitchel, Jno.		--	"	1-12-15	Dartmoor Prison
Mitchell, Ezekiel		Me.	"	12-12-14	Dartmoor Prison
Mitchell, Joseph	Private	21st Inf.	"	6-10-13	
Mitchell, Peter	"	N.Y.	"	1-22-15	
Mitchell, Thos.	Sailor	Essex	Killed	3-28-14	
Mitchell, Will'm	Private	21st Inf.	Died	7-28-13	
Mitchell, Wm.	"	--	"	8-4-13	Quebec Prison
Moffitt, Thomas	"	3rd Art.	"	3-19-13	
Moin, James	"	12th Inf.	"	--	
Molton, Michael C.	1 Lt.	39th Inf.Tenn.Mil.	Killed	2-37-14	
Moncure, John Daniel	Surgeon	At. Ft. George	Died	10-7-13	
Monell, Peter		Lawrence	Killed	9-10-13	
Money, Thomas M.	Private	20th Inf.	Died	--	
Monroe, John		N.Y.	"	1-2-15	Dartmoor Prison
Montgomery, Alen		--	Killed	1-22-13	
Montgomery, Alexander	Surgeon		"	1-22-13	
Montgomery, Jno		N.Y.	Died	2-24-13	Dartmoor Prison
Montgomery, John		Mass.	"	2-24-14	Dartmoor Prison
Montgomery, Lemuel P.	Major	39th Inf.Tenn.Mil.	Killed	3-27-14	
Montgomery, William	Private	22nd Inf.	Died	2-14-14	
Moody, Blood	"	4th Inf.	"	1814	
Moody, John S.	Corporal	4th Inf.	"	--	
Moody, Josiah	Private	4th Inf.	"	9-25-13	

Moore, Charles	Private	22nd Inf.	Died	Dec. 1814	
Moore, Edward	Seaman	Saratoga	Killed	9-11-14	
Moore, George		Mass.	Died	3-30-15	Dartmoor Prison
Moore, Henry		N.Y.	"	1-14-14	Dartmoor Prison
Moore, John	Surg.Mate	Ky. Mil.	"	11-12-13	
Moore, John, Jr.	Private	Art.	"	12-8-13	
Moore, Josiah	"	22nd Inf.	"	--	
Moore, Josias	"	--	"	9-11-13	Quebec Prison
Moore, Mark	"	O.	"	1812	
Moore, Perkins	Seaman	Eagle - Lake Champ	Killed	9-11-14	
Moore, Robt.	1 lt.	Tenn.	"	11-9-13	
Moore, Thomas	Private	41st Inf.	Died	1-8-14	
Moore, Thomas	"	4th Inf.	"	6-16-13	
Moore, William	"	16th Inf.	"	12-1-12	
Moorehead, Samuel	"	Pa. Mil.	"	9-22-14	
Moorehouse,	"	34th Inf.	"	9-14-14	
Moores, Jacob B.	"	11th Inf.	"	5-16-13	
Moran, Nicholas	"	Ky. Mil.	"	5-17-13	
Morehead, Samuel	"	Pa. Mil.	"	9-22-14	
Morehouse, Gideon	"	25th Inf.	"	8-21-13	
Morel, Peter	Sailor	SS Niagara	Killed	9-10-13	
Morell, Peter	"	Niagara	"	12-31-13	
Morgan,	Captain	Mass.	Died	3-16-14	Chatham
Morgan, Alexander	Private	15th Inf.	"	1-10-14	
Morgan, George	Seaman	N.Y.	"	June 1814	Stapleton Prison
Morgan, Lodowick	Major	1st Rifles	Killed	8-12-14	
Morrell, Joseph	Private	Art. Reg.	Died	10-29-14	
Morrell, Joseph	"	Art. Reg.	"	10-29-14	
Morrill, Enoch	"	9th Inf.	"	1-2-14	
Morrill, Joseph	"	Art.	"	1814	
Morrill, Samuel	"	31st Inf.	"	10-12-14	
Morris,	"	8th Inf.	"	June 1814	
Morris, Henry	"	10th Inf.	"	--	
Morris, James		Md.	"	3-26-15	Dartmoor Prison
Morris, John	Private	Ky. Mil.	"	1-1-15	
Morris, John	"	7th US Inf.	"	1-8-14	
Morris, Robert	Ensign	13th Inf.	"	10-13-12	
Morris, Walter	Private	7th US Inf.	"	5-24-14	
Morrison, John	"	12th Inf.	"	3-1-14	
Morrison, John C.	Captain	--	Killed	5-5-13	
Morrison, Robert	Private	19th Inf.	Died	11-2-13	
Morrison, Thomas		Md.	"	10-1-13	Dartmoor Prison
Morrison, Wm.		Md.	"	12-14-14	Dartmoor Prison
Morrison, Wm.		8th Inf.	"	9-30-14	
Morse, Joshua		25th Inf.	"	10-6-13	
Mortimer, Balden, Jr.	Private	14th Inf.	"	10-19-14	
Mory, James	"	9th Inf.	"	10-27-14	
Moslaird, Reuben	Sailor	Mass.	"	11-25-13	Chatham
Moules, James	Private	17th Inf.	"	1-15-15	
Moulton, Richard	"	11th Inf.	"	9-25-14	
Mountain, Michael B.	"	2nd Art.	"	4-22-14	
Mounter, Joseph	Seaman	Alligator	"	7-1-14	
Moutle, Charles		Conn.	"	2-21-15	Dartmoor Prison
Mozengo, James F.	Private	2nd Art.	"	--	
Mualab, Archibald	"	34th Inf.	"	9-15-14	
Mudge, Charles	"	21st Inf.	"	8-19-14	

Mudge, Joseph		--	Died	12-30-14	Dartmoor Prison
Mullard,	Private	1st Inf.	"	10-16-14	
Mullen, Lindsey	"	Ky. Mil.	"	9-29-13	
Muller, Solomon	"	23rd Inf.	"	10-4-14	
Munroe, Amara	"	25th Inf.	"	4-23-13	
Munroe, Samuel	"	3rd Art.	"	12-5-13	
Muncreef, Jno.	"	--	"	10-30-13	Quebec Prison
Mur, Elias L.	3 Lt.	4th Rifles	"	10-19-14	
Murdock, Thomas	Private	4th Rifles	"	12-21-14	
Murphy, Barney	"	7th US Inf.	"	3-9-14	
Murphy, John	Captain	Globe	Killed	9-4-14	
Murphy, John	Private	8th Inf.	Died	1-5-14	
Murray,		Ky. Vols.	Killed	11-22-12	
Murray, William (boy)	Boston Macedonian		Killed	10-30-12	
Mutry, Michael	Private	22nd Inf.	Died	1-1-14	
Musgrove, Job	"	Va. Mil.	"	12-24-14	
Myer, William		Champ. Squad	Killed	9-11-14	
Myers, George	Private	N.Y. Vols	Died	9-13-14	
Myers, Henry	"	1st Rifles	"	11-8-14	
Myers, John	"	30th Inf.	"	12-27-14	
Myers, Peter	"	22nd Inf.	"	1-7-14	
Myers, Solomon	"	5th Inf.	"	10-19-14	
Myrick, Azel	"	10th Inf.	"	Nov. 1813	
Narramore, Joel	Private	25th Inf.	Died	6-12-13	
Nash, Daniel		--	"	2-14-14	Dartmoor Prison
Nash, Daniel		Md.	"	2-24-15	Dartmoor Prison
Nash, William	2 Lt.	34th Inf.	Killed	8-1-13	
Nations, Frederick	Private	17th Inf.	Died	3-21-15	
Nay, John	"	Ky. Mil.	"	10-13-13	
Neal, Jeremiah	"	14th Inf.	"	1-15-15	
Neal, Joseph	"	9th Inf.	"	11-20-13	
Needham, Danl.	"	21st Inf.	"	Dec. 1814	
Nelson, Andrew	Seaman	Saratoga	Killed	9-11-14	
Nelson, Arthur	Private	4th Rifles	Died	11-30-14	
Nelson, George	Captain	6th Inf.	Killed	10-13-12	
Nelson, Robert	Private	32nd Inf.	Died	2-11-15	
Nelson, Samuel	Sailor	N.Y.	"	3-29-13	Chatham
Nevins, David	Private	6th Inf.	"	1-2-13	
Newbern, Benj.		N.Y.	"	11-15-13	Dartmoor Prison
Newcomb, Oliver	Sgt.	21st Inf.	"	1-31-13	
Newcomb, Remember	Private	9th Inf.	"	7-9-13	
Newcomb, Wm.	"	O.	"	1812	

Newell, Barston	Private	21st Inf.	Died	7-20-13	
Newland, Joel	"	Ky. Mil.	"	10-24-13	
Newman, Jacob	"	41st Inf.	"	1-4-15	
Newman, Thomas	"	Inf.Miss.Mil.	Killed	1815	
Newton, Joseph	Sgt.	15th Inf.	Died	11-9-12	
Nicholls, Silas S.	Corporal	23rd Inf.	"	5-24-14	
Nichols, A.	Private	33rd Inf.	"	10-3-13	
Nichols, Hugh	Sailor	N.C.	"	1-6-14	Chatham
Nichols, John H.	Private	11th Inf.	"	10-30-14	
Nichols, Moses	Lieut.	Drag.	"	12-5-13	
Nicholson, Benj.	Captain	--	"	4-27-12	
Nicholson, Benjamin	"	14th US Inf.	"	5-13-13	
Nickerson, Solomon	Private	21st Inf.	"	10-1-14	
Niel, Jeremiah	"	14th Inf.	"	1-15-15	
Nilson, John	Seaman	Alligator	"	7-1-14	
Nixon, George	Major	19th Reg.Pa.Mil.	"	1815	
Nixon, James	Private	Ky. Mil.	"	12-20-14	
Noggle, Michl.	"	5th Inf.	"	11-27-14	
Noggle, Peter	"	22nd Inf.	"	8-19-14	
Norberry, James	Mate	Saratoga	Killed	9-11-14	
Nordyke, Thos.		Essex	"	3-28-14	
Norgren, Chas. E.		Essex	"	3-28-14	
Norris, Benj.	Private	17th Inf.	Died	12-25-14	
Norris, Beverly	"	Ky. Inf.	"	10-31-14	
Norris, Jas.	"	14th N.Y. Vols.	"	8-30-14	
Norris, William	"	14th Inf.	"	1-21-15	
Norriss, Beverly	"	17th Inf.	"	12-24-14	
North, Zachariah	Corporal	19th Inf.	"	--	
Northrop, Gerskam	Private	25th Inf.	"	9-1-14	
Norton, Edw.	Sailor	Mass. - Frolick	"	9-29-14	Dartmoor Prison
Norton, Hugh	Private	23rd Inf.	"	7-25-14	
Norton, Obed	Sgt.	17th Inf.	"	12-9-14	
Norvel, Samuel	Private	12th Inf.	"	11-4-14	
Nott, Joseph	"	Ky. Mil.	"	8-1-13	
Noyes, Joseph	"	Lt. Art.	"	--	
O'Conner, John	Private	12th Inf.	Died	2-21-15	
Odenbaugh, Charles	"	22nd Inf.	"	4-22-13	
O'Donnel,	Marine	N.Y.	Killed	10-30-12	Macedonian
O'Flint, Elijah T.	Ensign	--	Died	9-17-14	
Ogden, James S.	Private	41st Inf.	"	10-20-14	
Oiler, George	"	14th Inf.	"	9-19-13	
Olcott, Abel	Sgt.	N.Y. Vols.	Killed	12-30-13	Black Rock
Older, John	Private	45th Inf.	Died	--	
Oliver, Joel	"	1st Inf.	"	--	
Oliver, Robert	"	10th Inf.	"	--	

Name	Rank	Unit	Status	Date	Notes
Olmstead, Alden	Private	41st Inf.	Died	3-6-15	
Olmstead, Edward	1 Lt.	16th Inf.	Killed	11-11-13	
Omstead, Ezekiel	Private	25th Inf.	Died	8-22-13	
Ongrain, Jonas	Seaman	Constitution	Killed	12-29-12	
Onlow, Reuben	Private	Ky. Mil.	Died	3-20-14	
Opdike,	"	16th Inf.	"	12-23-13	
Oram, John	"	Va. Inf.	"	4-3-13	
Ord, John	"	22nd Inf.	"	7-5-14	
Ore, William	"	9th Inf.	"	12-11-13	
Ore, Edward	"	15th Inf.	"	Aug. 1813	
Osborn, S. M.	Lieut.	1st Reg.Miss.Vols.	Killed	8-30-13	
Osgood, John	Private	9th Inf.	Died	11-22-14	
Ostrander, Abram	"	22nd Inf.	"	6-28-13	
Ottinger, Charles	"	16th Inf.	"	4-15-13	
Otis, Rinson	"	21st Inf.	"	8-5-12	
Overbagh, Jeremiah	"	23rd Inf.	"	1813	
Overbok, Elias	"	6th Inf.	"	3-22-14	
Overt, George		N.H.	"	1-28-15	Dartmoor Prison
Overton, Thomas J.	1 Lt.	17th Inf.	Killed	1-22-13	
Owen, William	Captain	22nd Ga.Mil R.	Died	7-30-14	
Owens, Alex	Private	9th Inv.	"	7-31-14	
Pace,	Captain	--	Killed	12-23-14	
Packard, Israel	Private	21st Inf.	Died	Oct. 1813	
Packer, George	"	.21st Inf.	"	Oct. 1814	
Paestow, Joel	"	15th Inf.	"	12-12-12	
Page, Ebenezer	"	37th Inf.	"	3-12-15	
Page, Orsmus	"	11th Inf.	"	4-8-13	
Page, Lure	"	9th Inf.	"	12-8-13	
Paine, David	"	25th Inf.	"	--	
Paine, William	"	33rd Inf.	"	5-4-13	
Paine, William G.	"	14th Inf.	"	2-23-14	
Pair, Clement	Sailor	Me.	"	4-20-14	Chatham
Paisley, Wm.	Private	15th Inf.	"	--	
Palmer, James		N.H.	"	11-7-14	Dartmoor Prison
Palmer, John		N.H.	"	1814	Dartmoor Prison
Palmer, Hampton	Private	11th US Inf.	"	1814	
Palmer, Jno.		N.H.	"	11-17-14	Dartmoor Prison
Palmer, John Hampton	"	31st US Inf.	"	1814	
Palmer, William	"	22nd Inf.	"	2-13-14	
Palmer, Richard	"	17th Inf.	"	12-8-14	
Palmre, John Hampton	"	31st US Inf.	"	1812	
Pamfield, Thomas	"	2nd Art.	"	9-4-13	
Pangborne, David	"	23rd Inf.	"	2-10-13	
Panter, Joseph	"	2nd Art.	"	9-2-12	
Parager, James		Ida	"	1814	Dartmoor Prison
Pare, William	Private	22nd Inf.	"	1-6-14	
Parents, John	"	7th US Inf.	"	5-2-14	

Name	Rank	Unit	Status	Date	Place
Parish, Samuel		Va.	Died	4-1-15	Dartmoor Prison
Park, Rodger	Private	--	"	11-6-13	Quebec Prison
Parker, Aaron	"	9th Inf.	"	11-30-13	
Parker, Benj.	"	Art.	"	4-10-14	
Parker, Charles		N.Y.	"	1-30-14	Dartmoor Prison
Parker, Edw'd.	"	--	"	9-19-13	Quebec Prison
Parker, Farwell	"	3rd Art.	"	1-28-13	
Parker, Lola	Lieut.	--	"	11-4-14	Ft. Independence
Parker, Moses	Private	21st Inf.	"	10-25-13	
Parker, Sam'l.	Lieut.	Drag.	"	6-24-13	
Parker, Thomas		Md.	"	11-5-14	Dartmoor Prison
Parker, Wm.		N.Y.	"	11-26-14	Dartmoor Prison
Parker, Wm.		Va.	"	11-28-14	Dartmoor Prison
Parkhurst, Thomas	Private	11th Inf.	"	12-31-14	
Parks, Benjamin	"	11th Inf.	"	5-7-14	
Parks, David	"	4th Rfls.	"	May 1815	
Parks, James	"	30th Inf.	"	2-9-15	
Parmelee, Andrew	Seaman	Saratoga	Killed	9-11-14	
Parmer, Richard	Private	17th Inf.	Died	12-8-14	
Parmley, Andrew Y		Champ. Squad	"	9-11-14	
Parogay, Jos.		Mass.	"	11-24-14	Dartmoor Prison
Parrott, Abraham	Private	16th Inf.	"	11-13-13	
Parslow, Henry		N.Y.	"	1814	
Partile, Alfred	Private	8th Inf.	"	--	
Paselo, Henry	Corporal	Art. Reg.	"	9-10-14	
Patrick,		--	Killed	1-22-13	
Pattee, Dummer	Lieut.	Art.	Died	--	
Patten, Edward	Sailor	Baltimore	"	4-21-14	Chatham
Patten, G. I. Mass.	"	Enterprise	"	--	
Patten, John		Pa.	"	1814	Dartmoor Prison
Patterson, Erastus	Private	11th Inf.	"	--	
Patterson, John	"	22nd Inf.	"	Dec. 1813	
Patterson, Mark	"	9th Inf.	"	6-1-13	
Pattison, John	"	22nd Inf.	"	1813	
Paul, Jno.	"	14th N.Y. Vols.	"	9-15-14	
Paul, John	"	Pa. Vols.	"	9-25-14	
Paul, Jonathan	"	S.C.	"	3-10-15	Dartmoor Prison
Paul, Simeon	"	--	"	8-25-13	Quebec Prison
Paulk, Moses	"	Ky. Mil.	"	2-16-15	
Peabody, Moses	"	9th Inf.	"	Apr. 1813	
Peach, Isaac	"	14th Inf.	"	2-8-15	
Pearsall, Samuel	"	Ky. Mil.	"	7-21-13	
Peasley, David	"	14th Inf.	"	12-21-12	
Peck,	Lieut	--	Killed		Fort Niagara
Peck, Henry	Private	11th Inf.	Died	9-27-14	
Peck, Patrick	"	Miss. Drag.	"	12-30-14	
Pecken, George	"	21st Inf.	"	11-27-14	
Peckham, Thomas	"	Conn.	"	3-15-15	Dartmoor Prison
Peebles, James	"	Ky. Mil.	"	5-5-13	
Penton, William	"	2nd Art.	"	12-18-13	
Pontz,	Lieut.	--	Killed	8-5-12	
Perez, Lincoln	Private	21st Inf.	Died	9-25-14	
Perigo, Joel	"	Mass.	"	11-4-14	Dartmoor Prison
Perkans, James	"	4th Inf.	"	10-6-14	
Perkins, Daniel	"	9th Inf.	"	5-29-13	

Name	Rank	Unit	Died/Killed	Date	Location
Perkins, Horatio	Private	9th Inf.	Died	5-27-13	
Perkins, James	"	4th Inf.	"	10-6-14	
Perkins, Jas.	"	Mass.	"	11-3-14	Dartmoor Prison
Perkins, John	Corporal	3 & 11th Inf.Vt.Mil.	"	4-24-13	
Perkins, John	Private	11th Inf.	"	--	
Perkins, Joseph	Syren	Mass.	"	1814	Dartmoor Prison
Perkins, Lyman	Private	25th Inf.	"	8-6-13	
Perkins, Moore	Seaman	Brig. Beagle	"	9-11-14	
Perry, Nathan	Private	0.	"	1813	
Perry, Philo	Sgt.	11th Inf.	"	10-18-13	
Perry, Saml.	Private	33rd Inf.	"	12-20-13	
Peter, Will'm	"	2nd Art.	"	9-1-13	
Peters, Aaron		Mass	"	1-30-14	Dartmoor Prison
Peters, Nelson	Seaman	Lawrence	"	12-31-13	
Peters, William	Private	2nd Art.	"	--	
Peterson, Aaron	Com.	--	"	1-14-14	Dartmoor Prison
Peterson, Andrew	Private	5th Inf.	"	10-19-14	
Peterson, Saml.		Pa.	"	12-9-14	Dartmoor Prison
Pettengell, Josiah		Mass.	"	10-7-14	Dartmoor Prison
Pettigrew,	Corp.	8th Inf.	"	June 1814	
Petty, Ezeikel	Private	21st Inf.	"	11-4-14	
Petty, John	"	13th Inf.	"	10-22-12	
Philbrick, David	"	33rd Inf.	"	10-6-14	
Philbrick, Jno.	"	21st Inf.	"	12-18-14	
Philbrook, Jonathan	"	21st Inf.	"	--	
Philips, Joshua	"	23rd Inf.	"	9-17-14	
Phillippi, Abraham	"	7th Co.Pa.Mil.	"	1-19-12	
Phillips, George W.	"	Art.	"	Sept. 1813	
Pickinpaw, Jacob F.	"	15th Inf.Reg.Pa.Mil.	"	4-5-14	
Pierce, Benoni	Captain	19th US Inf.	Killed	12-17-12	
Pierce, John	Private	Art.	Died	8-23-14	
Pierce, Joseph	"	5th Inf.	"	--	
Pierce, Joseph	"	--	"	1-29-15	
Pierce, Samuel		R.I.	"	3-12-14	Dartmoor Prison
Pierce, Zadock	Private	10th Inf.	"	Sept. 1813	
Pierson, John	"	US Army	"	1-2-14	
Pierson, John	"	N.Y. Mil.	"	1-2-14	
Pike,	General	USS Madison	Killed	--	
Pike, Artemus	Private	N.Y. Mil.	Died	1814	
Pike, David	"	2nd Art.	"	--	
Pike, Zebulou M.	Brig. Gen.		Killed	4-27-13	
Pillsbury, Tobias	Private	34th Inf.	Died	9-6-14	
Pingree, James	"	11th Inf.	"	4-21-15	
Pinkerman, John	"	17th Inf.	"	11-12-14	
Pinkham, David	Sailor	Mass.	"	1-6-14	Chatham
Pinkham, Ephra		Mass.	"	9-25-14	Dartmoor Prison
Pinkham, Ephraim		Me.	"	9-25-14	Dartmoor Prison
Piper, Jonathan	Private	21st Inf.	"	--	
Place, Freeman	"	41st Inf.	"	11-30-14	
Place, George	"	25th Inf.	"	11-13-14	
Place, John	Sailor	Hornet	Killed	2-24-13	
Plaisted, Oliver	Private	11th Inf.	Died	4-4-13	
Plumby, Robt.	Private	12th Inf.	"	1-3-14	
Plumley, John		22nd Inf.	"	7-25-14	
Poe,	Adj.	Pa. Vols.	Killed	11-11-13	
Poe, Thos.	Adj.	--	"	7-25-14	

Name	Rank	Unit/Ship	Status	Date	Location
Pohig, Charles	Seaman	Lawrence	Killed	12-31-13	
Pointer, Thos.	Private	3rd Rifles	Died	2-20-15	
Polhill, Thomas R.W.	Captain	Ga. Mil.	"	11-24-14	
Pollard, George	Ida	Mass.	"	1814	Dartmoor Prison
Pollard, George		Mass.	"	11-23-14	Dartmoor Prison
Pollard, Hopewell	Midshipman	Chesapeake	Killed	6-1-13	
Pollard, John		S. America	Died	11-23-14	Dartmoor Prison
Ponsland, William	Sailor	Mass.	"	4-3-14	Chatham
Pool, Garrit G.	Private	13th Inf.	"	3-17-13	
Pool, Hiram	"	Lt. Art.	"	6-25-12	
Pool, Luke	"	21st Inf.	"	--	
Pool, Thomas	"	33rd Inf.	"	--	
Pope, Jeremiah		Upper Montclair,N.J.	"	1814	
Pope, Moses	Private	5th Inf.	Killed	11-19-14	
Pope, Samuel		Upper Montclair,N.J.	Died	1814	
Porter, Charles		--	"	1-14-14	Dartmoor Prison
Porter, Ezra		25th Inf.	"	12-3-12	
Porter, Gideon		R.I.	"	3-22-15	Dartmoor Prison
Porter, John	Private	20th Inf.	"	2-19-15	
Porter, John	Captain	--	Killed	1814	New Orleans
Porter, Joshua	Private	13th Inf.	Died	3-12-14	
Post, Christopher	"	25th Inf.	"	12-2-12	
Post, Peter	Seaman	Saratoga	Killed	9-11-14	
Potter, John		Pa.	Died	10-5-14	Dartmoor Prison
Potter, Jno.	Private		"	12-7-13	Quebec Prison
Potter, William	Sailor	Mass.	"	5-24-14	Chatham
Potters, G. I.		Mass.	"	10-7-14	Dartmoor Prison
Potters, Jno.		Pa.	"	10-5-14	Dartmoor Prison
Pottle, Dudley	Private	11th Inf.	"	8-25-14	
Potts, Francis	"	20th Inf.	"	10-31-14	
Potts, Jacob	"	20th Inf.	"	--	
Poulter, Joseph	"	Ky. Mil.	"	1-19-15	
Powell, John	Sailor	Essex	Killed	3-28-14	
Powell, Joseph	Private	16th Inf.	Died	--	
Powell, Stephen	"	10th Inf.	"	12-15-13	
Powers, Edmund		Champ. Squad	Killed	9-11-14	
Powers, John	Private	16th Inf.	Died	6-22-14	
Powers, William	"	13th Inf.	"	10-22-13	
Pratt, Benj.	"	--	"	--	Quebec Prison
Pratt, Ivory	"	13th Inf.	"	Nov. 1813	
Pratt, Nathl.	"	--	"	7-23-13	Quebec Prison
Pratt, Walter	"	--	"	9-15-13	Quebec Prison
Pregone, Jno	"	14th Inf.	"	11-22-14	
Preist, Bartholomew	"	21st Inf.	"	8-27-14	
Prentiss, Henry	"	9th Inf.	"	--	
Prentiss, Manasseh	Captain	N.Y. Mil.	"	1814	Sacketts Harbor
Preston, Lemuel	Private	4th Inf.	"	10-4-13	
Price, James C	Captain		Killed	1-22-13	
Price, Joseph	Private	11th Inf.	"	7-5-14	
Price, Richard	2 Lieut	28th Inf.	Died	11-11-13	
Price, Stephen	Private	11th Inf.	"	8-5-14	
Price, William	"	Lt. Art.	"	--	
Price, William	"	16th Inf.	"	--	
Price William	"	13th Inf.	"	1-5-15	
Prien, John	"	22nd Inf.	"	10-23-14	
Priest, Bartholomew	"	21st Inf.	"	9-27-14	

Prince, Joseph	Private	4th Inf.	Died	12-27-14
Prior, James	"	5th Inf.	"	1-13-15
Pritchard, James	"	O	"	1813
Pritchett, Joshua	"	Lt. Art.	"	--
Probert, Thomas	Corporal	10th Inf.	"	5-5-14
Probst,	Lieut.	Drag.	"	2-26-14
Probst, George	Private	Lt. Drag.	"	2-18-14
Procter, Shadrack	Private	2nd Art.	"	9-21-13
Provance, Benjamin	"	Pa. Vols.	"	1-11-14
Pryor, John	"	14th Inf.	"	11-22-14
Pullom, John	"	Ky. Mil.	"	12-29-14
Pully, Robt.	"	12th Inf.	"	11-22-14
Puntney, Aquilla		O. Mil.	Killed	9-15-12
Putnam, Daniel	Private	--	Died	8-24-13
Putnam, Elisha	"	21st US Inf.	"	1-7-14
Pyatt, Nathan	"	6th Ky. Mil.	"	12-4-12

Qarren, Nathaniel	Seaman	Enterprise	Killed	9-5-13	
Quarles, Stores	Private	Ky. Mil.	Died	2-22-15	
Quarles,	Captain	--	"	1-24-14	
Querean, Benj.	Sailmaker	U.S. Madison	Killed	4-24-13	
Quimby, John	Private	9th Inf.	Died	7-6-13	
Quion, Joseph		Mass.	"	2-23-15	Dartmoor Prison

Raffity, John	Private	Ky. Mil.	Died	1-14-15
Ralls, Green	"	Ky. Mil.	"	2-2-15
Ramlez, Huthun	"	22nd Inf.	"	11-2-14
Ramsey, William	"	3rd Rifles	"	3-19-15
Ramsdell, Joel	"	25th Inf.	"	12-7-13
Ramsdell,Valentine		O. Mil.	"	--
Ramsdell, William	Private	11th Inf.	"	6-30-14
Randall, Amos	"	11th Inf.	"	Nov. 1813
Randall, Aguila A.	"	Mich. Vols.	Killed	9-14-14
Rankin,		1st Reg. Miss.Vols	"	8-30-13
Ranlay, Nathan	Private	22nd Inf.	Died	11-2-14
Ransom, Moses	"	11th Inf.	"	4-20-13
Ransom, Samuel	"	23rd Inf.	"	7-25-14

Name	Rank	Unit	Status	Date	Notes
Rantz, Nan	Private	13th Inf.	Died	11-11-13	
Rasmussen, Andrew E.Sr.	Captain		Killed	7-22-13	In Navy
Rasom, Joseph		Me.	Died	3-2-15	Dartmoor Prison
Rawson, Samuel	Private	N.Y. Mil.	"	1814	
Ray, Jared	Sailor	N.Y.	"	1-4-14	Chatham
Ray, John	Private	Ky. Mil.	"	12-22-14	
Raynolds, William	Major	3rd O. Vols	"	11-12-14	
Rea, John P.	Sailor	Alligator	"	7-1-14	
Read, Francis	Private	9th Drag.	"	1-8-14	
Read, James	"	Ky. Mil.	"	12-20-14	
Read, James	Seaman	--	Killed	10-30-12	
Read, James	"	Frig. Const.	"	8-20-12	
Read, Jeremiah	Private	7th US Inf.	Died	4-3-14	
Read, John	"	19th Drag.	"	2-5-14	
Ready,	Lieut.	--	Killed in capture of Guerrier		
Reardon, John	Private	Lt. Drag.	Died	1-8-15	
Reardon, Paul	"	Art.	"	11-30-14	
Reams, Bartlet	"	7 US Inf.	"	3-10-15	in New Orleans
Redman, Joseph	"	13th Inf.	"	1-3-13	
Reding, William	"	17th Inf.	"	--	
Reed, Benjamin	"	5th Inf.	"	--	
Reed, David		Mass	"	11-14-14	Dartmoor Prison
Reed, Isaac	Private	--	"	8-4-13	Quebec Prison
Reed, Jas.	"	15th Inf.	"	12-28-14	
Reed, Moses	"	--	"	--	
Reed, Robert	"	17th Inf.	"	--	
Reed, Samuel	"	9th Reg.	"	10-27-14	
Reed, Solomon	"	25th Drag.	"	2-21-15	
Reed, Wm.	Maj.Gen.	Pa. Mil.	"	6-15-13	
Reese, Alexander	Private	15th Inf.	"	11-6-12	
Reid, John	"	12th Inf.	"	12-10-13	
Reid, Jonathan	"	6th Inf.	"	1-27-13	
Reid, Robert	Captain	--	"	1814	
Renow. Benja		Fr. W.I.	"	11-16-14	Dartmoor Prison
Rennie, Nicholas T.	Purser	Alligator	"	7-1-14	
Rerick, John	Private	23rd Drag.	"	9-28-13	
Reynolds, Isaac P.	"	41st Inf.	"	1-18-15	
Reynolds, Isham	"	Ky. Inf.	"	10-31-14	
Reynolds, James	Surg.Mate	--	Killed	8-16-12	
Reynolds, Jethro	Private	1st Rifles	Died	June 1814	
Reynolds, John	"	20th Inf.	"	--	
Reynolds, John	"	Lt. Drag.	"	4-2-15	
Reynolds, Trueman	"	1st Rifles	"	4-16-14	
Reynolds, William	"	25th Inf.	"	12-3-13	
Rhea, John	"	24th Reg.	"	9-12-13	
Rheams, Bartley	"		"	10-3-15	
Ribero, John	Seaman	Brig.Beagle	"	9-11-14	
Rice, Asahel	Private	11th Inf.	"	6-6-12	
Rice, John	"	19th Inf.	"	--	
Rice, Thomas		Mass.-Galvador	"	2-15-14	Dartmoor Prison
Rice, Leonard	"	Rifles	"	11-13-14	
Rice, Samuel	"	45th Inf.	"	--	
Rich, John	"	Lt. Art.	"	3-4-13	
Richards, Edw. I.	"	15th Inf.	"	12-20-13	
Richards, John	"	38th Inf.	"	3-15-15	

Name	Rank	Unit	Status	Date	Notes
Richards, Nehennah		--	Killed	12-14-14	at New Orleans
Richardson, Ailsae	Private	Ky. Mil.	Died	6-4-14	
Richardson, Amos	"	38th Inf.	"	1-12-15	
Richardson, Jason	Sgt.	9th Drag.	"	1-27-15	
Richey, David	Corporal	Ky. Mil.	"	2-14-15	
Richey, Saml.	Private	22nd Inf.	"	--	
Richmond, Anthony	Corporal	25th Inf.	"	1-12-15	
Rickard, John J.	Private	Lt. Art.	"	6-25-13	
Ricker, John	"	22nd Inf.	"	11-15-14	
Riclor, Christian	"	14th Inf.	"	Nov. 1814	
Ridgeley, Daniel B.	2 Lt.		"	1814	
Riley, John O.	Private	23rd Inf.	"	9-6-14	
Rinevon, Benjamin		W. Ind.	"	11-16-14	Dartmoor Prison
Ring, Jonathan	Private	45th Inf.	"	--	
Ringwood, Thomas	"	41st Inf.	"	10-24-14	
Riol, David	"	10th Inf.	"	9-21-14	
Ripley,		23rd Inf.	"	11-5-14	
Ripley, Wm.	Private	23rd Inf.	"	11-5-14	
Rippley, John	Sailor	Essex	Killed	3-28-14	
Risdon, John		Md.	Died	2-14-15	Dartmoor Prison
Rising, Samuel	Private	Lt. Drag.	"	1-25-14	
Risley, Horace		N.Y.	"	May 1813	Dartmoor Prison
Ritchie,	Captain	Art.	Killed	11-11-13	
Ritchie, Samuel	Private	Art.	Died	1-16-14	
Ritchie, Samuel		O.	"	1815	
Ritchie, John	Captain	Art.	Killed	7-25-14	
Rix, James	Private	11th Drag.	Died	5-8-13	
Rix, Thomas		Va.	"	1-22-14	
Roach, Moses	Private	15th Inf.	"	1813	
Roads, Anderson	"	20th Reg.	"	6-1-15	
Roaply, John	Sailor	N.Y.	"	1-4-14	
Robenson, James		Mass.	"	4-1-15	Dartmoor Prison
Robenson, Joseph		Me.	"	3-2-15	Dartmoor Prison
Robenson, Samuel		Pa.	"	12-9-14	Dartmoor Prison
Robenson, Samuel		Mass.	"	2-15-15	Dartmoor Prison
Robenson, William		--	"	4-18-15	Dartmoor Prison
Roberson, Graham	Private	Ky. Mil.	"	10-19-12	
Roberts, Francis		Spain	"	2-7-15	Dartmoor Prison
Roberts, Hiram	Private	17th Inf.	"	1-13-15	
Roberts, John	N.Y.- Marine	Macedonian	Killed	10-30-12	
Roberts, John	Private	7th US Inf.	Died	4-5-14	
Roberts, Samuel	"	29th Inf.	"	--	
Robertson, Frank		Spain	"	2-7-14	Dartmoor Prison
Robertson, James	General		"	9-1-14	On Duty
Robertson, Joseph	Private	36th Inf.	"	--	
Robertson, Saml.		Mass.	"	2-15-15	Dartmoor Prison
Robbins, David	Private	Ky. Mil.	"	12-14-14	
Robins, Seth S	"	11th Inf.	"	8-15-14	
Robinson, Archibald	"	17th Inf.	"	11-12-14	
Robinson, Jas.	Corporal	36th Inf.	"	--	
Robinson, Levi	Private	11th Inf.	"	3-12-13	
Robinson, Nathaniel	"	US Inf.	"	10-22-14	
Robinson, Will	"	21st Inf.	"	7-16-13	
Robinson, William	"	19th Inf.	"	10-26-14	
Robinson, William	"	3rd Art	"	--	
Rochford, Will'm	"	3rd Art	"	May 1813	

Rodgers,	Private	8th Inf.	Died	June 1814	
Rodgers, Luke	"	N.C.	"	11-12-14	Dartmoor Prison
Rodgers, William	"	O. Mil.	"	12-3-15	
Roe, Jonas	"	Lt. Drag.	"	9-1-13	
Roff, Moses	"	Art.	"	--	
Roger, Filley	Sgt.	Ky. Mil.	"	1-23-15	
Rogers, Benjamin	Corporal	11th Inf.	"	--	
Rogers, Levi	Surgeon	19th Inf.	"	4-4-15	
Rogers, Robert	Sgt.	21st Inf.	"	--	
Rogerson, R.	Midshipman	Alligator	"	4-1-14	
Roll, William	Private	11th Inf.	"	6-13-14	
Rolls, Abijah	"	Ky. Mil.	"	11-27-14	
Ronan, George	Ensign	1st&54th Inf.	Killed	8-15-12	
Ropes, Daniel	Sailor	Mass.	Died	2-16-13	
Roosevelt, Thomas Wilton	Lieut.	N.Y. Inf.	Killed	9-4-14	at Fort Erie
Root, Austin,	Sgt.	11th Inf.	Died	1-10-13	
Root, Jno.	Private	--	"	8-23-13	Quebec Prison
Rooth, James		Conn.	"	12-29-14	Dartmoor Prison
Rose, Henry	Private	5th Inf.	"	--Prisoner in Halifax	
Rose, John	Seaman	Lawrence	Killed	12-31-13	
Rose, John	Gunner	" Adm.Perry's Flagship	"	9-10-13	In Battle
Rosebraugh, John	Private	22nd Inf.	Died	Dec. 1813	
Ross, David	"	22nd Inf.	"	--	
Ross, John	"	11th Inf.	"	9-27-14	
Ross, John E.	"	Co. Art.	"	1-1-14	
Ross, Thomas	"	23rd Inf.	"	1-17-15	
Rotter, John	Sailor	Maryland	"	5-9-13	Chatham
Roundy, Ralph	Private	4th Inf.	"	2-10-15	
Row, Benjamin	"	Lt. Art.	"	8-14-13	
Rowe, Joseph	Mate	Preble	Killed	9-11-14	
Rowland,	Private	39th Drag.	Died	10-19-14	
Rowley, Reuben	"	Lt. Drag.	"	11-13-14	
Rucker, Julius	Sgt.	Ky. Mil.	"	2-7-15	
Rue, John	Private	41st Inf.	"	9-1-14	
Rufus, Tenant	"	25th Inf.	"	--	
Rugg, Josiah	"	4th Inf.	"	11-22-13	
Rumley, Elisha	"	8th Inf.	"	1-31-14	
Rumble, Jacob	"	4th Rifles	"	--	
Rumny, Caseman	"	10th Inf.	"	12-9-13	
Rumsey, Aaron	"	11th Inf.	"	3-10-15	
Rundell, Charles	"	7th Inf.	"	5-24-14	
Runk, George W.	1 Lieut.	6th Inf.	"	9-7-14	
Runnells, John	Private	Art.	"	7-4-14	
Runyan, Israel	"	3rd Art.	"	9-29-13	
Russell, Benjamin	"	33rd Inf.	"	--	
Russell, Henry	N.Y. Mil.		"	4-2-14	Prisoner of War
Russell, Thos.		Essex	Killed	3-28-14	
Ryan, Joseph	Private	Rfls.	Died	6-30-12	

Name	Rank	Unit	Status	Date	Prison
Sackett, Elijah	Lieut.	--	Died	4-7-13	
Sago, Jacob	Seaman	Constitution	Killed	8-20-12	
Salesbury, Joseph		Mass.	Died	13-14-15	Dartmoor Prison
Salisbury,	.	2nd US Art.	Killed	10-30-12	
Salisbury, Simon	Private	23rd Inf.	Died	9-11-14	
Salvadore, Oliver	Q.M.	Alligator	"	7-1-14	
Samler, John	Private	13th Inf.	"	Oct. 1812	
Samborn, Jno. L.	"	--	"	7-23-13	Quebec Prison
Sanburn, Benjamin	"	13th Inf.	"	12-1-14	
Sanburn, Simeon	"	11th Inf.	"	4-3-13	
Sandborn, Geo. W.	"	11th Inf.	"	7-26-14	
Sanders, George	"	Ky. Mil.	"	1-5-15	
Sanders, Wait	"	29th Inf.	"	9-20-14	
Sanders, Williams B.	"	Ky. Mil.	"	9-17-13	
Sanderson, Abel	"	11th Inf.	"	8-25-14	
Sargent, James	"	4th Inf.	"	--	
Sargent, Jotham	"	3rd Art.	"	--	
Saul, Frances		Mass.	"	10-20-14	Dartmoor Prison
Sauls, Solomon	Private	US Inf.	"	10-15-14	
Saunders, Charles	Sailor	Va.	"	3-25-14	Chatham
Saunders, Elisha	Captain	N.Y.	Killed	10-13-12	
Saunders, John	Private	33rd Inf.	Died	12-25-13	
Saunders, Nathan	"	21st Inf.	"	--	
Saunders, Norman	"	2nd Art.	"	Oct. 1812	
Saunders, Wait	"	29th Inf.	"	9-20-14	
Saunders, Wm.		Md.	"	1-16-15	Dartmoor Prison
Saunders, William		Me.	"	1-16-14	Dartmoor Prison
Savage, Saml.	Private	22nd Inf.	"	10-30-14	
Savary, J.	"	4th Inf.	"	8-25-14	
Savil, Edward	"	9th Inf.	"	11-11-13	
Sawyer, Jacob		R.I.	"	10-25-14	Dartmoor Prison
Sawyer, Jed	Private	R.I.	"	10-25-14	Dartmoor Prison
Sawyer, Jonathan	Sailor	Me.	"	3-24-14	Chatham
Sawyer, Reuben	Private	25th Inf.	"	12-19-13	
Saxton, Arthur	"	3rd Inf.	"	Mar. 1815	
Sayres, James	"	15th Inf.	"	9-9-13	
Sayro, Seely	Sgt.	12th Reg.US Inf.	"	1-3-15	
Scarlet, Wm.	Sailor	Alligator	"	7-1-14	
Schelding, Henry		--	"	1-24-14	Dartmoor Prison
Schoffield, Wm.	Private	7th Inf.	"	--	
Schofield, Joseph	"	25th Inf.	"	--	
Schofield, Thos.	"	25th Inf.	"	1-7-15	
Schriner, George Michael	"	Pa. Mil.	"	12-5-15	
Scills, Miles	"	35th Inf.	"	12-14-14	
Scott, Andrew	"	15th Inf.	"	7-15-13	
Scott, David	"	17th Inf.	"	--	
Scott, Henry	Sailor	Baltimore	"	3-24-14	Chatham
Scott, Hugh	Private	2nd Art.	"	--	
Scott, John	"	25th Inf.	"	8-23-14	
Scott, Jno	"	25th Inf.	"	8-23-14	
Scott, William	"	12th Inf.	"	11-3-14	
Scudding,	Sailor	Me.	"	1-19-14	Dartmoor Prison
Scudding, Sam		Me.-Siro	"	1814	Dartmoor Prison
Sealand, James	Private	3rd Art.	"	6-10-13	
Sealy, Jeremiah	"	Art.	"	9-13-14	
Sealy, Reuben	"	9th Inf.	"	--	

Sealsmon, Thomas	Private	7th Inf.	Died	4-13-14	
Sean, Terrival	--		Killed	12-14-14	At New Orleans
Seapach, John	Me.		Died	2-7-15	Dartmoor Prison
Searle, Robert	Private	6th Inf.	"	1-10-14	
Searle, Thomas	"	25th Inf.	"	2-5-15	
Seaton, James P.	"	11th Inf.	"	2-26-13	
Sebor, Jacob	Sgt.	6th Inf.	"	--	
Secusa, Jacob C	N.Y.		"	12-7-14	Dartmoor Prison
Sedinger, Casper	Private	16th Inf.	"	6-16-13	
Seeley, Jeremiah	"	Art.	"	9-14-14	
Seeney, King	"	Art.	"	3-27-13	
Segourney,	Officer	Scorpion	Killed	7-18-13	(about)
Selden, Samuel	Adj.	3rd Reg.N.H.Mil	Died	1814	
Sellock, John	Seaman	Saratoga	Killed	9-11-14	
Sellers, James	Essex		"	3-28-14	
Sellick, Benjamin	Private	13th Inf.	Died	10-13-12	
Senior, John	"	2nd Art.	"	11-12-13	
Seth, William C.	Adj.	Md. Mil.	"	1815	
Severance, Jonathan	Private	11th Inf.	"	11-1-14	
Sevier, John	General	--	"	9-24-15	On military mission for P.Madison
Sew, Jacob	N.Y. Vols.		"	1814	Dartmoor Prison
Seydan, Jacob	Private	Lt. Drag.	"	1-8-14	
Seymour, Garrard	"	Art.	"	8-26-14	
Sharbley, Philip	Corporal	Marines-Lawrence	Killed	12-31-13	
Sharer, Philip S	Ensign	17th Inf	"	1-22-13	
Sharey, Daniel	Private	21st Inf.	Died	11-19-14	
Sharp, Delany	"	3rd Art.	"	Aug. 1813	
Sharp, John	Marine-Ticonderoga		Killed	9-11-14	
Shattuck, Rufus	Private	13th Inf.	Died	9-16-13	
Shaver, George	"	--	"	7-26-13	Quebec Prison
Shaw, Nathl	"	12th Inf.	"	10-24-14	
Shaw, Spencer	"	Art.	"	10-19-14	
Shaw, Wm.	"	Pa.	"	10-17-14	Dartmoor Prison
Shaw, William	Argus-Pa.		"	1814	Dartmoor Prison
Shebeg, Jacob	Private	16th Inf.	"	--	
Sheets, Jacob	"	19th Inf.	"	5-20-13	
Sheldon, Henry	--		"	1-24-14	Dartmoor Prison
Sheperd, John	Surgeon	O.	"	1812	
Shephard, John	Lake Champ.		Killed	9-11-14	
Shepherd, Henry	Seaman	Phila.	"	10-25-12	
Sheppard, James	Private	14th Inf.	Died	1-22-13	
Shelhouse, Martin G.	Corporal	O.	"	1813	
Shells, Henry	Private	14th N.Y. Vols	"	10-15-14	
Sherman, Silas, Jr.	Captain	8th Reg.R.I.Mil.	"	4-4-14	
Sherrer, Robert	Private	12th Inf.	"	4-25-14	
Shertine, Joshua	"	2nd Inf.	"	1-2-15	
Sherwood, Joel	"	29th Inf.	"	5-24-15	
Shewell, William	"	22nd Inf.	"	12-22-13	
Shields, Patrick	"	7th US Inf.	"	5-26-14	
Shillingford, James	"	16th Inf.	"	12-11-13	
Shivers, Burton P.	"	7th US Inf.	"	6-10-14	
Shores, John	"	9th Inf.	"	11-10-13	
Shouse, Abram	"	Ky. Mil.	"	4-13-13	
Shuilliff, Isaac	"	21st Inf.	"	June 1813	
Shumate, Julius R.	Surgeon	22nd Inf.	Killed	9-1-13	

Name	Rank	Unit		Date	Location
Shumman, Druses	Private	11th Inf.	Died	2-22-13	
Shute, David		Mass.	"	3-4-15	Dartmoor Prison
Shute, Joseph	Private	Art.	"	10-27-14	
Sibley, Artemas	Ensign	4th Inf.	Killed	8-16-12	
Sickles, John W.	Private	16th Inf.	Died	3-24-15	
Sidebottom, Wilson	"	17th Inf.	"	3-18-15	
Sidney, John P.	Sgt.	Frenchtown	Killed	1-22-13	
Sill, Washington	Private	15th Inf.	Died	9-9-13	
Silver, David	"	4th Inf.	"	8-12-14	
Silver, David	"	14th Inf.	"	--	
Silver, John	"	4th Inf.	"	1-24-15	
Simerson, Isaac		N.Y.	"	11-20-14	Dartmoor Prison
Simkins, Gilbert	Private	23rd Inf.	"	6-23-15	
Simons, Abraham		O. Mil.	"	--	
Simons, Daniel		Mass.	"	1-28-15	Dartmoor Prison
Simons, Ebenezer		--	"	1-12-15	Dartmoor Prison
Simmon,		--	"	1-20-15	Dartmoor Prison
Simmons, Richard	Private	Miss. Mil.	"	8-30-14	
Simmons, Simon	Seaman	Surprise	Drowned	4-5-15	
Simonds, Elizur	Private	31st Inf.	Died	9-22-14	
Simonds, Jonathan	"	21st Inf.	"	8-17-14	
Simonds, Proctor	Sailor	--	"	3-19-14	Chatham
Simpson, Gilbert	Private	2nd Reg.E.Tenn.Vols.	"	11-3-13	
Simpson, Isaac	Sailor	Invincible-N.Y.	"	12-20-14	Dartmoor Prison
Simpson, James	Private	Ky. Mil.	"	6-25-13	
Simpson, John	Captain		Killed	1-22-13	
Simpson, William	Private	45th Inf.	Died	11-23-14	
Sims, Benjamin	"	30th Inf.	"	1-14-14	
Sims, Daniel	"	16th Inf.	"	10-17-14	
Sinamon, Dan		Mass.	"	1-23-15	Dartmoor Prison
Sinclair, Jacob	Private	--	"	9-19-13	Quebec Prison
Singleton, James	General	16th Brig.V.M.	"	2-14-15	
Singlewurst, James	Private	33rd Inf.	"	12-18-13	
Sisson, Alex	Lieut.	--	"	11-28-12	
Skelton, William	Private	9th Inf.	"	10-20-14	
Skinner, Ebenezer	Sailor	Mass.	"	3-24-14	Chatham
Skinner, James A.	Private	8th Inf.	"	10-30-13	
Skinner, Walter	Corporal	3rd Art.	"	Sept. 1813	
Sloan, Daniel	Private	Ky. Mil.	"	5-5-13	
Slawson, David	"	13th Inf.	"	6-24-14	
Small, Edward	"	11th Inf.	"	8-1-14	
Smart, Alexander	"	1st Rfls,	"	12-31-13	(about)
Smart, David	Seaman	N.Y.	"	June 1814	Stapleton Prison
Smart, John	"	Saratoga	Killed	9-11-14	
Smart, Wm.		Va.	Died	12-5-14	Dartmoor Prison
Smeal, Peter	Private	16th Inf.	"	4-5-14	
Smit, Nichol		Va.	"	12-8-14	Dartmoor Prison
Smith, Alexander	"	34th Inf.	"	11-26-13	
Smith, Alexander	""	Art.	"	1-13-14	
Smith, Andrew		--	"	3-5-15	Dartmoor Prison
Smith, Anthony	Private	15th Inf.	"	3-29-14	
Smith, Arthur W	Purser	Borer	Killed	9-11-14	
Smith, Byrd	Brig.Gen.	W. Tenn, Mil.	Died	2-19-15	
Smith, Caleb	Seaman	Constitution	Killed	10-30-12	
Smith, Chad	Private	25th Inf.	Died	12-5-13	

Smith, Charles	Private	21st Inf.	Died	10-11-14	
Smith, Daniel	Lieut.	Artillery	"	—	
Smith, Daniel	Private	5th Inf.	"	12-18-12	
Smith, Daniel	Private	34th Inf.	"	9-19-14	
Smith, David	Corporal	Ky. Mil.	"	9-1-13	
Smith, Elias	Private	4th Inf.	"	3-10-14	
Smith, Harry	Private	11th Inf.	"	4-22-13	
Smith, Harry	Private	11th Inf.	"	5-10-13	
Smith, Hezikiah	Private	31st Inf.	"	4-3-14	
Smith, James	Sailor	Mass.	"	4-24-14	At Chatham
Smith, James	Private	20th Inf.	"	8-29-13	
Smith, Jon	Private		"	4-28-13	Quebec Prison
Smith, John	Seaman	Lawrence	Killed	12-31-13	
Smith, John	2nd Lt.	Globe	"	11-1-13	
Smith, John	Private	21 Inf.	Died	10-28-14	
Smith, Joel	Private	17th Inf.	"	12-25-14	
Smith, Joel	Private	9th Inf.	"	11-11-13	
Smith, Jonathan	Private	34th Inf.	"	April 1814	In Prison
Smith, Joshua	Private	41st Inf.	"	12-22-14	
Smith, Josiah	Corporal	21st Inf.	"	—	
Smith, Matthew	Private	Ky. Mil.	"	1-31-15	
Smith, Michael	Private	22 Inf.	"	1-6-14	
Smith, Nathan	Private	Lt. Art.	"	March 1815	
Smith, Nicholas	Private	Va.	"	12-8-14	Dartmoor Prison
Smith, Orange	Private	25th Inf.	"	—	
Smith, Owen	Private	25th Inf.	"	Nov. 1813	
Smith, Phineas	Private	11th Inf.	"	4-24-13	
Smith, Reuben	Private	25th Inf.	"	9-23-14	
Smith, Richard	Private		"	4-14-15	Dartmoor Prison
Smith, Robert	Private	2nd Art.	"	8-13-14	
Smith, Roberts	Private	Art.	"	11-26-14	
Smith, Robert	Private	2nd Lt. Drags.	"	8-31-13	
Smith, Samuel	Seaman	Saratoga	Killed	9-11-14	
Smith, Samuel D.	Seaman	Globe	"	11-1-13	
Smith, Samuel	Private	Ky. Mil.	Died	5-18-14	
Smith, Schelding		New York	"	1-14-14	Dartmoor Prison
Smith, Stephen	Private		"	9-5-13	Quebec Prison
Smith, Stephen	Private	9th Inf.	"		
Smith, Terrence	Private	17th Inf.	Killed	1-21-13	In Battle of River Raisin
Smith, Thomas O.	Private	1 Reg.Tenn.Mil.	Died	1-20-15	
Smith, Wm.	Private	22nd Inf.	"	9-11-14	
Smith, Wm.	Private		"	7-16-13	Quebec Prison
Smith, William	Private	11th Inf.	"	6-10-14	
Smith, William	Private	22nd Inf.	"	9-11-14	
Smith, William	Private	Lt. Drag.	"	9-21-14	
Smith, William	Private	Art.	"	6-10-14	
Smith, William	Mate	Essex	Killed	7-3-14	
Smith, William	Private	7th Inf.	Died	4-28-14	
Smith, William	Mate	Essex	Killed	3-28-14	
Smith, W. W.	Lieut.		"	11-11-13	

Smith, William W.	Lieut.	Lt. Art.	Killed	11-11-13	
Snell, Theodore		R.I.	Died	3-16-15	Dartmoor Prison
Snead, Jacob	Private	1 Rfls.Va.Mil.	"	11-22-14	
Snediger, Moses	Private	U.S. Inf.	"	3-25-14	
Sneed, Zeakle	Private		"	2-4-13	Quebec Prison
Snow, Mark	Seaman	Constitution	Killed	12-29-12	
Snow, Nathaniel	Private	34th Inf.	Died	9-30-14	
Snow, William	Private	12th Inf.	"	12-13-13	
Snowden, Robert	Sgt.	U. S. Inf.	"	12-31-14	
Snyder, George	Private	Art.	"	7-25-14	
Snyder, Michael	Private	Va. Mil.	"	1-27-15	
Snyder, Peter	Private	2nd Art.	"	Nov.1812	
Somerville, Robert M.	1st Lt.	39th Inf. Tenn.	Killed	3-27-14	
Somes, William	Private	4th Inf.	Died	8-8-14	
Southoomb, John	Capt.	Privateer-Lottery	Killed	2-8-13	
Souther, E.	Private	4th Inf.	Died	12-26-14	
Southerland, Wm.			Killed	11-4-16	At New Orleans
Southworth, Luther	Private	11th Inf.	Died	1-31-14	
Sovereign, Jonathan	Private	11th Inf.	"	11-1-14	
Sparks, James		7th Inf.	"	4-18-14	
Sparks, Thomas	Private	25th Inf.	"	11-25-13	
Spear, Edward	Lt.	Rangers	Killed	5-24-15	
Spear, Elijah	Private	25th Inf.	Died	10-12-13	
Spear, Samuel	Private	3rd Ky. Mil.	"	12-3-12	
Spence, Willis	Private	3rd Ky. Mil.	"	2-1-15	
Spencer, Ambrose	Capt.		"	7-25-14	
Spencer, Danl.	Private	3oth Inf.	"	11-20-13	
Spencer, George	Private		"	1814	
Spencer, Jasper G.	Private	41st Inf.	"	2-2-15	
Spencer, Joseph	Private	41st Inf.	"	10-14-14	
Spencer, Wm. S.	Private	20th Inf.	"	12-20-12	
Sperdy, Richard		Va.	"	11-3-14	Dartmoor Prison
Sprague, Eleakin	Private	11th Inf.	"	11-23-14	
Sprague, Ephraim	Private	17th Inf.	"	1-25-15	
Sprague, Jeremiah	Private	11th Inf.	"	7-5-14	
Springer, John	Sgt.	9th Inf.	"	1-27-15	
Spurtin, John	Private	7th Inf.	"	4-1-14	
Spurtin, Topley	Private	7th Inf.	"	6-20-14	
Squibs, Silas	Com.		"	3-17-15	Dartmoor Prison
Sroffe, Emanuel	Private	19th Inf.	"	1-6-15	
Stacy, Stephen		Mass.	"	3-16-15	Dartmoor Prison
Stagg, Abraham	Private	15th Inf.	"	10-12-14	
Staird, Isaac	Private		"	2-8-13	Quebec Prison
Stanfield, John	Private	Ky. Mil.	"	12-23-14	
Stanley, Joseph	Private	25th Inf.	"	12-17-13	
Stanley, Nathaniel			"	1814	Sackett's Harbor
Stanley, Nathaniel		2nd Reg.Drahy Mil.	"	1814	
Stansbury, John	Lieut.	Ticonderoga	Killed	9-11-14	
Stanton, Smilie	Private	4th Inf.	Died	11-10-14	
Stanwood, Jeremiah		Mass.	"	3-20-15	Dartmoor Prison

Name	Rank	Unit	Status	Date	Notes
Staples, Henry	Gunner	Wasp	Killed	9-1-14	
Staples, Joseph	Private	9th Inf.	Died		
Staples, Joshua	Private	14th N.Y.Vols.	"	9-15-14	
Staten, Joseph	Private	Ky. Inf.	"	5-5-13	
Staton, Robert	Sailor	Champ.Squad	Killed	9-11-14	
Stearnes, Nath.	Private	34th Inf.	Died		
Stedham, William	Private	6th Inf.	"	5-7-14	
Steeds, John	Sgt.	Co. Art.	"	10-15-14	
Steel, Job	Private	N. Y. Mil.	"	Feb.1813	
Steel, John		Ireland	"	12-15-14	
Steel, Joseph	Private	15th Inf.	"	1-8-14	
Steel, Wm.	Seaman	Alligator	"	7-1-14	
Stephen, Moses	Private	25th Inf.	"	Jan.1815	
Stephens, Archibald	Private	15th Inf.	"	3-22-15	
Stephens, George	Private	Ky. Mil.	"	2-25-15	
Stephens, James	Private	22nd Inf.	"	1-15-14	
Stephens, Thomas	Seaman	Saratoga	Killed	9-11-14	
Stephens, Williams	Private	14th Inf.	Died	9-29-14	
Stephenson, Thos.	Private	6th Inf.	"	11-4-13	
Stephenson, William	Private	14th Inf.	"	1-17-15	
Sternburg, Christian	Private	17th Inf.	"	12-10-14	
Sternis, William	Com.		"	3-15-14	Dartmoor Prison
Stevens, Henry	Private	25th Inf.	"	6-6-13	
Stevens, James	Private	4th Inf.	"	6-30-15	
Stevens, Mathew	Private	16th Inf.	"	9-30-14	
Stevens, Matthew	Private	16th Inf.	"	10-24-14	
Stevens, Samuel	Private	11th Inf.	"		
Stevens, Thomas	Seaman	Saratoga	"	9-11-14	
Stevens, William	Private	14th Inf.	"	9-29-14	
Stevens, William	Sgt.	10th Inf.	"		
Stevenson, John	Private	Ky. Inf.	"	5-5-13	
Stewart	Private	22nd Art.	Killed	10-30-12	
Stewart, Aaron	Sgt.	21st Inf.	Died	7-16-13	
Stewart, Abraham	Private	15th Inf.	"	1-14-14	
Stewart, John	Private	21st Inf.	"	4-24-15	
Stewart, Robert	Private	20th Inf.	"	5-3-14	
Stewart, Simeon	Private	1st Rfls.	"	9-17-14	
Stewart, William	Private	12th Inf.	"	11-6-13	
Stifford, Elisha	Private	9th Inf.	"	12-24-13	
Stickney, Abijah	Private	3rd Art.	"	9-30-14	
Stiles, John		Md.	"	12-15-14	Dartmoor Prison
Stiles, Samuel	Private	N.Y. Reg.	"	1814	
Stocker, Adam	Private	Pa. Mil.	"	6-27-14	
Stocking, Horace	Private	25th Inf.	"	11-30-13	
Stoddard, Amos	Major	1st Art.	"	5-9-13	
Stone, Artemas	Private	40th Inf.	"	6-21-14	
Stone, Isaac	Col.	N.Y. Mil.	"	Aug.1814	
Stoner, John	Private	O 13th Inf.	"	2-28-15	
Storm, William	Private	3rd Ky. Mil.	"	12-1-12	
Story, Nathan	Private	25th Inf.	"	11-10-14	

Stougton, Russell	Private	25th Inf.	Died	9-23-14	
Stout, David	Private	22nd Inf.	"	9-17-14	
Stout, Jerry	Sailor	Alligator	"	7-1-14	
Stout, Wash G.	Private		"	1812	
Stow, John	Sailor	Harlequin	"	1-5-15	Dartmoor Prison
Stow, John		Md.	"	1-5-15	Dartmoor Prison
Stow, Lewis		N. Y.	"	12-21-14	Dartmoor Prison
Stow, Lewis		Zickler, N.Y.	"	1814	Dartmoor Prison
Stow, Lewis		Conn.	"	11-21-14	Dartmoor Prison
Stranghorn, Hugh	Seaman	High Flyer	Killed	Dec.1812	
Stratton, Robert	Marine	Eagle	"	9-11-14	
Straul, John		Me.	Died	1-20-15	
Straw, John M.	Private	11th Inf.	"	3-26-13	
Strawmat, William	Private	Ky. Mil.	"	2-13-15	
Strawmut, John	Private	Ky. Mil.	"	3-15-15	
Strong, John	Private	29th Inf.	"	9-26-14	
Strout, John		Me.-Harlequin	"	1814	
Strout, John			"	1-20-14	Dartmoor Prison
Studdy, Richa		Virginia	"	11-3-14	Dartmoor Prison
Stultz, Adam	Private	19th Inf.	Killed	5-5-13	
Stults, Jacob	Private	19th Inf.	Died	11-29-14	
Sturgis, William	1st Lt.	22nd Inf.	Killed	7-25-14	
Sturtivant, Abijah	Private	33nd Inf.	Died	10-4-14	
Sudert, David	Cpl.	U. S. Inf.	"	11-25-14	
Sullivan, Nathan	Private	5th Inf.	"	10-26-14	
Summer, Samuel	Private	9th Inf.	"	7-21-13	
Summers, John	Private	15th Inf.	"	10-29-14	
Sutton, David	Private	12th Inf.	"	12-6-13	
Sutton, Martin		Mass.	"	2-22-15	Dartmoor Prison
Swallow, Zephan	Private	12th Inf.	"		
Swain, Abm	Private	16th Inf.	"	9-27-13	
Swain, Paul	Private	14th Inf.	"	11-28-12	
Swan, Ensign		1st Reg.Miss.Vols.	Killed	8-30-13	
Swany, Edward	Private	1st Art.	Died	5-23-14	
Swart, Cornelius	Private	25th Inf.	"	11-11-13	
Swartz, Daniel	Private	Pa. Mil.	"	1-7-15	
Swasey, John	Sgt.	21st Inf.	"	Dec.1812	
Sweet, William	Private	25th Inf.	"	3-16-15	
Swift, John	Brig. Gen.		Killed	7-14-14	In U.C.at Newark
Swinny, Stephen	Private	Art.	Died	10-30-13	
Sykes, Ethelbred		S.S. Lawrence	Killed	12-31-13	
Sylhamamer, John		Scorpion	"	12-31-13	
Sylhamaner, John		Scorpion	"	9-10-13	
Sylver, John	Private	4th Inf.	"	1-24-15	
Symmes, Benjamin	Private	9th Inf.	Died	1-27-15	
Symmes, John C.	Judge	O	"	1814	
Symonds, Eleazoer	Private	31st Inf.	"	9-22-14	
Symonds, Sylvester	Private	4th Inf.	"	1-24-15	
Soypher, James	Private	13th Inf.	"	8-14-13	

Taft, Artemus	Private	25th Inf.	Died		
Tailor, J. B.		N. Y.	"	12-2-14	Dartmoor Prison
Tandy, William	Private	21st Inf.	"	12-12-12	
Tankerly, Wm.	Private	39th Inf.	"		
Tarbell, Joseph	Captain	U.S.N.	"	11-24-15	
Tarr, Danl.	Private	14th Inf.	"	1-19-15	
Tarr, William	Private	9th Inf.	"	6-8-13	
Tarrent, Richard	Private	Lt. Drag.	"	12-31-13	
Tate, John	Private	12th Inf.	"	1812	
Tanerdale, Darins	Private	25th Inf.	"		
Taylor, Ebenezer	Private	Co. Art.	"	Dec.1813	
Taylor, E.	Private	25th Inf.	"	10-26-13	
Taylor, Elisha	Private	25th Inf.	"	10-28-14	
Taylor, Hezekiah	Private	5th Inf.	"	11-30-12	
Taylor, John	Midshipman		Killed	10-30-12	
Taylor, John	Private	38th Inf.	Died	1-11-15	
Taylor, John	Private	4th Inf.	"	12-27-14	
Taylor, John	Private	32nd Inf.	"	2-14-15	
Taylor, John	Sailor	President	Killed	6-24-12	
Taylor, John	Private	7th Inf.	Died	5-23-14	
Taylor, John	Private	14th Inf.	"	2-21-13	
Taylor, John B.	Private	N. Y.	"	12-2-14	Dartmoor Prison
Taylor, Nathaniel	General	Tenn. Mil.	"	1815	
Taylor, Peter	Private	25th Inf.	"	11-1-14	
Taylor, Redding	Private	10th Inf.	"	3-20-15	
Taylor, Solomon	Private	Ky. Mil.	"	3-3-15	
Taylor, William	Private	4th Inf.	"	Aug.1813	
Taylor, William			Killed	9-4-12	At Ft. Harrison
Tempre, Samuel	Private	1st Inf.	Died	9-11-14	
Tenny, Samuel	Private	21st Inf.	"	11-11-14	
Tenney, Samuel	Private	21st Inf.	"	1-18-15	
Terheun, Albert	Private	15th Inf.	"		
Terhew, Albert	Private	15th Inf.	"	1-13-15	
Terry, Thos.	Private	Essex	Killed	3-28-14	
Terry, Wm.			Died	2-15-13	Dartmoor Prison
Tevis, Peter	Cpl.	17th Inf.	"	1-10-15	
Thacker, James	Private	74th Reg.Va.Mil.	"	1815	Drowned
Thaye, William	Private	9th Inf.	"		
Thayer, Nathaniel	Private	23rd Inf.	"	8-23-14	
Thatson, Stephen	Sailor	Mass.	"	3-26-13	Chatham
Thelis, James	Seaman	Globe	Killed	11-1-13	
Theophilus	Private	4th Inf.	Died	9-24-14	
Think, Deodrick	Marine	Ticonderoga	Killed	9-11-14	
Thomas, Abraham		Conn.	Died	7-23-14	Dartmoor Prison
Thomas, Enoch	Private	3rd Art.	"	12-31-13	
Thomas, Henry		Mass.	"	2-21-15	Dartmoor Prison
Thomas, Henry Clarence		Mass.	"	1814	Dartmoor Prison
Thomas, John	Private	4th Inf.	"	12-23-13	
Thomas, John		N. Y.	"	10-25-14	Dartmoor Prison
Thomas, Leonard	Private	16th Inf.	"	3-14-15	

Thomas, Togatt	Private Granville	Died	3-18-14	Dartmoor Prison
Thomas, Thomas	Private O. Mil.	"	6-6-14	
Thomas, Uriah	Sailor on Paul Jones-Conn.	"	7-23-14	Dartmoor Prison
Thompson,William	Private 19th Inf.	"	5-5-13	
Thompson, Josiah	Private 9th Inf.	"	11-30-14	
Thompson	Midshipman U. S. Madison	Killed	4-24-13	
Thompson, Benj.		Died	2-1-15	
Thompson, Moses		"	1-21-14	
Thompson	Midshipman	Killed	4-8-13	
Thompson, Richard	Private 12th Inf.	Died	5-21-14	
Thompson, Thomas	Private 2nd Art.	"	4-4-14	
Thompson, William		"	4-18-15	Dartmoor Prison
Thompson, Benj. C.	Cpl. 42nd Inf.	"		
Thompson, Cornelius	Essex	Killed	3-28-14	
Thompson, Samuel	Private 2nd Art.	Died	12-14-13	
Thompson, Samuel	Private 6th Inf.	"	2-1-13	
Thornsby, Asa	Private 5th Inf.	"	10-26-14	
Thorp, Joel C.	Private Art.	"	7-14-14	
Thorp, John	Sailor Champ. Squad.	Killed	9-11-14	
Thurston, Ebenezer	Private 9th Inf.	Died	12-29-13	
Thurston, Joel	Private 23rd Inf.	"	8-30-13	
Tible, Richard	Private Rfls.	"		
Tidwell, William	Private Ky. Mil.	"	10-23-13	
Tilden, Joseph	" Co. Art.	"	10-6-13	
Till, Jas.	Private	"	8-31-13	Quebec Prison
Tilman, Asbon	Private 10th Inf.	"	12-11-13	
Timmon, M.	N. Y.	"	2-26-13	Dartmoor Prison
Timmons, Eli	Private 19th Inf.	"		
Timmons, Wm.	" 18th Inf.	"	5-2-14	
Tineman, Matthew	N. Y.	"	9-26-14	Dartmoor Prison
Tinney	Private 45th Inf.	"	9-20-14	
Tobby, Elijah	N. Y.	"	3-9-14	Dartmoor Prison
Tobey, Edward	Private 34th Inf.	"	11-15-14	
Tobias, Sterne	Private Ky. Inf.	"	3-10-14	
Tobie, Eleazer	N. Y.	"	3-9-14	Dartmoor Prison
Toby, Thomas	Private 4th Inf.	"	5-7-14	
Thomas, John		"	10-25-13	Dartmoor Prison
Tomkins, K.		"	11-13-14	Dartmoor Prison
Tompkins, Abraham	N. Y.	"	11-3-14	Dartmoor Prison
Tophouse, Sam	Ala.	"	2-13-13	Dartmoor Prison
Topping, Zopher	Private 19th Inf.	"	9-27-14	
Torns, Richard	Private 6th Inf.	"	1-31-14	
Torrey, Mellan	Private Lt. Drag.	"	8-1-14	
Totterson, Henry	Cpl. 6th Inf.	"		
Tottingham, Asa	Private 25th Inf.	"	May 1813	
Tower, Elisha	Private Art.	"	2-7-14	
Tower, H. B.	Private 9th Inf.	"	7-5-14	
Town, Joseph	Private 1 Rfls.Pa.Mil.	"	1815	
Townsend, Isaac	Private 11th Inf.	Killed	11-11-13	
Towson, Benjamin	Private 17th Inf.	Died	12-13-14	

Name	Rank	Unit	Status	Date	Notes
Tracy, Lycanius	Cpl.	23rd Inf.	Died	8-24-13	
Trafford, George	Private	21st Inf.	#		
Trask, Daniel	Private	9th Inf.	"	12-13-12	
Trask, Joseph	Private	21st Inf.	"	9-13-13	
Trask, Nehemiah	Private	4th Inf.	"	2-17-15	
Tranblifiete, John	Private	Lt. Art.	"		
Traver, George	Private	2nd Art.	"	11-4-14	
Travis, Joseph D.	Private	27th Inf.	"	4-26-15	
Trotter, James	Lt.	1st Reg.Ky.Drag.	"	11-13-13	
Trowbridge, Charles D.	Private	15th Inf.	"	3-26-13	
Trueman, Jonathan	Sailor	Me.	"	5-28-14	Chatham
Tubbs, Hazall	Private	13th Inf.	"	4-15-15	
Tucker, Josiah	Private	9th Inf.	"	11-27-13	
Tuell, Roderick	Private	Lt. Art.	"		
Tufts, William	Private	9th Inf.	"		
Turner, David		Mass.	"	2-21-15	Dartmoor Prison
Turner, John		Mass.	"	4-6-14	Dartmoor Prison
Turner, Stephen	1st Lt.	9th Inf.	"	7-25-14	
Turner,	1st Lt.	9th Inf.	Killed	11-11-13	
Tuttle, Charles	Sgt.	25th Inf.	Died	8-6-14	
Tuttle, Francis		Me.	"	11-24-14	Dartmoor Prison
Tuttle, Nathan	Private	11th Inf.	"	6-17-13	
Twigg, Daniel		Wasp	Killed	10-18-12	
Twils	Private	Lt. Art.	Died	9-30-14	
Twiss, Samuel	Private	3rd Art.	"	9-30-14	
Tyler, Joseph	Private	Ky. Mil.	"	1-16-15	
Tyre, William		Mass.	"	2-25-14	Dartmoor Prison
Ullery	Capt.		Killed	8-5-12	
Umberger, Michael	Private	2nd Reg.Pa.Mil.	Died	3-4-15	
Underwood, John	Private	U.S.Inf.	"	5-6-14	
Upraft, Thos.	Private	38th Inf.	"	1-27-15	
Updike, John	Private	16th Inf.	"	12-23-13	
Uselton, William	Private	U.S. Inf.	"	3-15-14	
Usher, Robert	Private	6th Ky. Mil.	"	11-3-12	
Vallandingham, George	Private	U. S. Inf.	"	2-11-14	
Vallany, John	Private	22nd Inf.	"	7-25-14	
Valleau, John	1st Lt.	13th Inf.	Killed	10-13-12	
Vance, David	Capt.	N.C. Mil.	Died	1813	
Vance, Robert	Private	Co. Art.	"	Aug.1814	
Vanderman, Conrod		O.	"		
Vandermere, Peter F.	Mate	Eagle	Killed	9-11-14	
Van Dyck, John	Private	Lt. Art.	Died	11-20-13	
Van Dyke, Thomas John	Capt.	Surg. 3Reg.Tenn.Vols.	"	12-27-14	
Van Horn, Jesse	Private	15th Inf.	"	10-10-14	
Van Horne, Isaac, Jr.	Captain	19th Inf.	Killed	8-4-14	
Van Huys, Isaac	Capt.	3rd Reg.N.J. Mil.	Died	12-28-15	
Vanituyl, Amos	Private	13th Inf.	"	Feb.1813	
Vankanst, Nicholas	Private	13th Inf.	"	11-11-13	
Van Kirk, Thomas	Private	25th Inf.	"	9-11-13	
Vanlamp, Henry	Seaman	Surprise	"	4-5-15	Drowned

Vanlear, Isaac	Private	16th Inf.	Died	12-3-14	
Van Loon, Nicholas	Private	16th Inf.	"		
Van Orden, B.	Private	15th Inf.	"	11-15-12	
Van Patten, Philip	Private		"	9-15-12	
Van Racke, Aaron	Private	15th Inf.	"	12-25-13	
Van Riper, Isaac	Private	15th Inf.	"		
Van Steuben, Peter	Dr.	4th Co.Pa.Mil.	"	1-28-14	
Vantassel, Albert	Private	13th Inf.	"		
Vantassel, Isaac	Private	13th Inf.	"	9-30-14	
Van Voorhis, J. V.	Dr.	54th Inf.	Killed	8-15-12	
Vassa, James			Died	1-8-15	Dartmoor Prison
Vaughan, John	Private	Co. Art.	"	7-4-13	
Vaughn, K.		L. I.	"	8-31-14	Dartmoor Prison
Vaughn, Nathaniel		R. I.	"	8-31-14	Dartmoor Prison
Vedder, Albert	Private	13th Inf.	"	10-1-12	
Veeder, Abraham	General	N. Y. Mil.	"	1-25-14	
Very, Daniel	Sailor	Mass.-Frolic	"	1-24-15	Dartmoor Prison
Vhraane, Jacob	Private	6th Inf.	"	3-1-14	
Vickery, Elijah	Private	Art.	"		
Villins, Darius		R. I.	"	2-25-15	Dartmoor Prison
Vinall, David	Private	34th Inf.	"	9-15-14	
Virgin, James		Mass.-Growler	"	1814	Dartmoor Prison
Virquis, James		Mass.	"	1-8-15	Dartmoor Prison
Vrooman, Adam S.	Private	13th Inf.	"	12-8-12	
Waddle, Jacob	Private	24th Inf.	"		
Wade, Henry	Private	25th Inf.	"	4-28-13	
Wade, Abington	Private	2nd Art.	"	8-18-13	
Waistcoot, Stulely	Private	6th Inf.	"	1-24-14	
Wait, Aaron	Private	9th Inf.	"	12-24-14	
Wait, William C.	Sgt.	11th Inf.	"	8-27-14	
Walbridge, Henry	Sgt.Major--Vt. Mil.		"	2-12-14	
Walis, John	Private	10th Inf.	"	12-31-14	
Walker, Benjamin	Private	16th Inf.	"	1-24-15	
Walker, Horatio	Sgt.	44th Inf.	"	1-20-15	
Walker, Nathl	Corp.	11th Inf.	"	8-8-13	
Walker, Philip	Private	17th Inf.	"	11-30-14	
Walker, William	Private	U.S. Inf.	"	4-4-14	
Walker, Seth S.	Capt.	0	"	1815	
Wallace, Charles D.	Private	15th Inf.	"	5-27-13	
Wallace, Ewell	Private	Ky. Mil.	"	5-5-13	
Wallace, John	Marine	Eagle	Killed	9-11-14	
Waller, John	Major	9th Reg.Va.Mil.	Died	8-17-15	
Wallter, Simon D.	Captain		Killed	8-4-14	
Walton, Thomas	Private	5th Inf.	Died	11-19-14	
Walton, Wm.	Private	25th Inf.	Killed	6-1-13	
Waltz, Danl.	Lieut.	19th Inf.	"	12-17-12	
Wamer, Simeon	Private	11th Inf.	Died	11-28-13	
Wendel, Alexander	Private	41st Inf.	"	2-7-15	
Wannemaker, Wm.	Private	1st Lt. Drag.	"	8-25-13	
Ward, Benjamin	Private	Art.	"		

Name	Rank	Unit		Date	Notes
Ward, Daniels	Private	Rfls.	Died	5-31-15	
Ward, John	"	4th Inf.	"	7-16-14	
Ward, Laban	Private	13th Inf.	"	1-26-13	
Ward, Thomas	Private	Frenchtown	Killed	1-22-13	
Ward, William H.	Private	Ky. Mil.	Died	6-17-13	
Ware, Michael	Private	23rd Inf.	"	1-13-15	
Ware, Peter	Private	1st Lt. Drag.	"	1-5-14	
Warner, Andrew E.	Capt.	39th Reg.	"	9-14-14	At N. Point
Warner, Asher	Private		"	6-20-13	From Battle Wounds Rec'd at Sodus Pt., N.Y.
Warner, Benjm.	Private	25th Inf.	"	Nov.1813	
Warner, Samuel	Private	16th Inf.	"	7-6-12	
Warren, John	Private	11th Inf.	"	10-3-14	
Warren, Samuel	Private		"	4-29-13	Chatham
Warren, Renson	Private	11th Inf.	"	8-22-13	
Warrick, James	Private	10th Inf.	"	12-11-14	
Warriets, James	Private	10th Inf.	"	12-22-14	
Warterbury, Ebenezer	Private	25th Inf.	"	7-4-13	
Washburn, Amos	Private	Lt. Art.	"	8-21-13	
Washburn, Ephraim	Privateer	On Dash	"	1-27-15	At sea
Washington, John	Seaman		Killed	4-6-15	Dartmoor Prison
Washington, Thomas C.	Private	Ky. Mil.	Died	2-22-15	
Waterman, Elijah	Private	6th Inf.	"	9-20-14	
Waters, John	Private	15th Inf.	"	11-22-13	
Waters, Kerwin	Midshipman	Enterprise	Killed	11-11-13	
Watkins, David	Private	7th Inf.	Died	6-7-14	
Watkins, Thomas	Private	U.S.Inf.	"	3-4-14	
Watson, Mathew	Private	2nd Art.	"	8-27-13	
Watterman, Elijah	Private	6th Inf.	"	9-22-14	
Watters, Samuel	Private	23rd Inf.	"		
Watts,	Master of Sails		Killed	11-28-12	
Watts,	Private	4th Inf.	Died	1814	
Watts, Isaac	Seaman	S.C.	"	June1814	
Watts, Robert	Private	38th Inf.	"	1-5-15	
Watts, Wm.	Private	4th Inf.	"	11-18-14	
Watts, William	Private	4th Inf.	"	12-13-14	
Wattles, Benj. P.	Private	27th Inf.	"	12-11-14	
Wattles, Simon D.	Capt.	23rd Inf.	Killed	8-15-14	
Wayne, Josh	Private		Died	10-6-13	Quebec Prison
Wayson, Thomas	Private	4 Rifles	"	1-25-15	
Wead, Scudder	Private	25th Inf.	"	9-29-14	
Weaver, Jacob	Private	Rifles Tenn.Vols.	"	1815	
Weaver, Michl	Private	12th Inf.	"	1-18-14	
Webber,	Sailor	Me.	"	3-4-13	Chatham
Weblev, Levi	Private	4th Inf.	"	11-15-14	
Webster, Joseph	Private	33rd Inf.	"	11-2-14	
Wedger, Joseph		Mass.	"	1-8-15	Dartmoor Prison
Weed, Daniel	Private	11th Inf.	"	2-21-13	
Weed, James	Private	11th Inf.	"	1-13-15	
Weed, John	Private	13th Inf.	#		
Weeks, James	Sailor	Mass.	"	4-14-14	Chatham

Name	Rank	Unit	Status	Date	Notes
Weeks, Moses	Private	35th Inf.	Died	11-19-14	
Weeks, Samuel	Private	23rd Inf.	"	9-27-14	
Weeks, Wait	Private	45th Inf.	"	11-25-14	
Weizer, John	Private	20th Inf.	"	1-5-15	
Wells, Capt.	Private	54th Inf.	Killed	8-15-12	
Wells, Alexander-Bui	Built Forts Used		Died	12-9-13	
Wells, Appleton	Private	N.Y. Mil.	"	3-7-13	In Service
Wells, Benjamin	Private	8th Inf.	"	11-9-14	
Wells, Caleb	Private		"	7-29-13	Quebec Prison
Wells, Daniel	Private	Sharpshooters	Killed	9-14-14	
Wells, John	Private	13th Inf.	Died	3-28-14	
Wells, Levi	Ensign	7th Inf.	Killed	1-22-13	
Wells, Stephen	Sgt.	25th Inf.	Died	10-5-14	
Wells, Thomas, Jr.	Private	17th Inf.	"	1-22-13	
Wells, William	Capt.-Com. At Ft.Dearborn		Massacred	8-15-12	
Welker, William	Private	O. Mil.	Died	1814	
Welsh, Lawrence	Private	7th U.S. Inf.	"	4-9-14	
Wentworth, Daniel	Private	Me. Mil.	"	7-4-15	
Wentworth, Edmund	Private	4th Inf.	"	1-14-14	
Wentworth, Jacob	Private	9th Inf.	"	1-1-14	
Wert, George	Private	N. H.	"	1-28-15	Dartmoor Prison
Wertz, Israel	Private	O	"	1815	
Wescott, William	Private	Va.	"	12-5-14	Dartmoor Prison
West, Georgie		Mil.-Harlequin	"	1814	Dartmoor Prison
West, John	Private	13th Inf.	"	10-25-13	
West, Keen	Private	34th Inf.	Killed	4-24-14	
Westley, Harp	Private	Ky. Mil.	Died	2-14-15	
West, Nathan	Private	11th Inf.	"	10-20-14	
Weston, Benjamin	Private	20th Inf.	"	3-1-14	
Weston, John	Private	21st Inf.	"	12-27-13	
Whatson, Scott	Private	20th Inf.	"	3-11-14	
Wheaton, Freeman	Private	22nd Inf.	"		
Wheaton, William	Private	4th Inf.	"	10-19-14	
Wheeler, Abithar	Private	11th Inf.	"	1-1-14	
Wheeler, Bryant	Private	10th Inf.	"	12-6-13	
Wheeler, Charles	Private	Ky. Mil.	"	1-6-15	
Wheeler, Cornelius	Private	9th Inf.	"	7-26-14	Of Wounds
Wheeler, Thomas	Private	9th Inf.	"	8-8-13	
Whidden, Tim	Private	21st Inf.	"	1-29-15	
Whiley, Saml.	Private	1st Inf.	"	12-15-06	
Whipple, Wm.	Private	9th Inf.	"	6-3-15	
Whiston, Francis	Private	9th Inf.	"	1-7-13	
White,			Killed on Chesapeake		
White, B.	Private	18th Inf.	Died	11-23-14	
White, David	Private	11th Inf.	"	10-29-14	
White, Ebenezer	Sailor	N. Y.	"	7-6-14	At Sacketts Harbor
White, George	Private	22nd Inf.	"	9-13-14	
White, Henry	Private	Ky. Inf.	"	5-5-13	
White, James	Carpenter - Argus		Killed	8-14-13	
White, John	Seaman	Saratoga	"	9-11-14	

White, John	Seaman	U.S. Ariel	Killed	9-10-13
White, John	Private	Ky. Mil.	Died	12-27-14
White, John	Private	1st Art.	"	3-3-14
White, John	Private	16th Inf.	"	6-29-14
White, John	Private	11th Inf.	"	10-29-14
White, John	Private	5th Inf.	"	4-5-13
White, John	Mate	S.S.Ariel	Killed	12-31-13
White, John	Private	Art.	Died	1-29-15
White, Joseph	Private	38th Inf.	"	1-15-15
White, William		Essex	Killed	3-28-14
White, Wm. A.	Sailor	Chesapeake	"	6-1-13
Whitehead, Danl.	Private	25th Inf.	Died	Nov.1813
Whitehead, Mahlon	Cpl.	6th Inf.	"	
Whitemore, John	Private	4th Inf.	"	10-27-14
Whitham, Jno.		N.H.	"	1-14-15 Dartmoor Prison
Whitham, John		Me.-Harlequin	"	1814 Dartmoor Prison
Whiting, Jason		9th Inf.	"	11-28-13
Whitlock	Private	8th Inf.	"	June1814
Whitman, John	Private	11th Inf.	"	11-8-14
Whittier, Isaac	Sgt.	21st Inf.	"	
Wiggins, Joshua	Private	Ky. Mil.	"	12-26-14
Wight, Oliver	Private	21st Inf.	"	11-25-12
Wilcox, Nathaniel	Private	11th Inf.	"	12-6-12
Willcox, Joseph M.	1st Lt.	3rd Inf.	Killed	1-15-14
Wilcocks	Lt. Col.		"	9-6-14
Wilder, Ephraim	Sgt.	Lt. Drag.	Died	6-6-13
Wile, Conrad	Private		Killed	1814
Wiley, Henry	Private	23rd Inf.	Died	11-13-14
Willard, Moses V.	Private	11th Inf.	"	7-25-14
Wilkinson, Willett	Private	41st Inf.	"	1-22-15
William, Carey	Private	1st Drag.	"	6-12-11
William, Dickerson	Lt.	Ky. Mil.	"	11-1-13
Williams	Captain		Killed	at Ft. Erie
Williams, Abner	Private	Lawrence	"	12-31-13
Williams, Alexander J.	Captain	Art.	"	8-15-14
Williams, O.	2nd Lt.	Privateer	Killed	
Williams, Charles	Com.		Died	3-10-15 Dartmoor Prison
Williams, Edward	Sailor	Pa.	"	3-6-14 Chatham
Williams, Edward		Va.	"	3-26-14 Dartmoor Prison
Williams, Francis	Sailor	Mass.	"	8-16-13 Chatham
Williams, Henry	Cpl.	18th Inf.	"	9-18-12
Williams, Isaac	Private	13th Inf.	#	
Williams, James	Private	22nd Inf.	"	1-14-14 Dartmoor Prison
Williams, James		Mass.	"	10-27-14 Dartmoor Prison
Williams, James			"	2-1-15 Dartmoor Prison
Williams, Jerome	Seaman	Saratoga	Killed	9-11-14
Williams	Captain		"	Battle at Ft. Erie
Williams, Jno.	Capt.	Marines	Died	11-9-12
Williams, John	Private	16th Inf.	"	12-13-14
Williams, John	Private	Ky. Mil.	"	9-26-12

Name	Rank	Unit	Fate	Date	Place
Williams, Joseph		Gay Head	Died	2-1-15	Dartmoor Prison
Williams, Lot	Private	Lt. Drag.	"	11-24-14	
Williams, Samuel		Mass.	"	3-17-15	Dartmoor Prison
Williams, Seth		N. H.	"	1-17-14	Dartmoor Prison
Williams, Thomas	Comm.		"	3-20-14	Dartmoor Prison
Williams, William		Wash, D.C.	"	10-22-14	Dartmoor Prison
Williamson, John	Lt.		Killed	1-22-13	
Williamson, John	Private	1st Rfles.	Died	10-3-13	
Williamson, Andrew	Private	Co. Art.	"	11-13-14	
Williamson, William	Sailor	Essex	Killed	3-28-14	
Willis, William	Private	23rd Inf.	Died		
Wilmer, James P.	Lt.	Essex	Killed	3-28-14	
Wilson, James	Private	6th Inf.	Died	12-2-12	
Wilson, James	Private	8th Inf.	"	1-6-14	
Wilson, James	Private	3rd Art.	"	5-15-13	
Wilson, Mace		Eagle	Killed	9-11-14	
Wilson, Saml.	Private	18th Inf.	Died	12-5-14	
Wilson, William	Private	6th Inf.	"	7-6-14	
Willson, Wm. B.	Private	6th Inf.	"	9-9-14	
Wiltse, I. B.	Private	29th Inf.	"	7-25-14	
Wiman, Gardner	Captain	14th Reg.N.Y.Mil.	"	12-27-12	
Winchell, Shalah	Private	25th Inf.	"	9-27-14	
Winchester, Ichabod	Private	1st Art.	"	7-19-13	
Winchester, Richard	Sailor	Mass.	"	3-4-13	Chatham
Wing, Asa	Private	4th Inf.	"	11-7-14	
Wingate, Ansil	Private	34th Inf.	"		
Wingate, Jeremiah	Private	3rd Art.	"	11-30-13	
Winship, James	Seaman	Eagle	Killed	9-11-14	
Winstrom, John			"	1-8-15	N. Orleans
Wisl,Scudder	Private	25th Inf.	Died	9-19-14	
Wiscoat, David	Private	34th Inf.	"	9-8-14	
Wiseman, Paul	Private	12th Inf.	"	12-8-12	
Withans, Joseph	Private	9th Inf.	"	7-5-14	
Wolf, George	Corp.	O. Mil.	"	12-6-13	
Wolfenton, Robert	Private	22nd Inf.	"	3-31-13	
Wolfinger, John	Private	22nd Inf.	"	11-30-13	
Wood, E. D.	Lt. Col.		Killed	9-17-14	
Wood, James	Private	22nd Inf.	Died		
Wood, John	Musician	- Eagle	Killed	9-11-14	
Wood, John	Private	24th Inf.	Died	Oct.1813	
Woods, Harris	Private	2nd Art.	"		
Woods, John	Captain	Tenn. Vols.	"	4-19-15	
Woodburn, Robert	Private	Pa. Vols.	"	9-4-14	
Woodbury, James	Q.M.-Chesapeake		Killed	6-1-13	
Woodcock, Isaiah	Private	9th Inf.	Died	9-2-14	
Wooders, Stephen	Private	Ky. Mil.	"	2-18-15	
Woodman, Robert	Private	14 N.Y. Vols.	"	9-4-14	
Woodward, Amasa	Private	9th Inf.	"	7-7-13	
Woodward, Israel	Private	23rd Inf.	"		
Woodward, Silas	Private	Ky. Mil.	"	8-10-13	

Woodworth, William	Private	3rd Reg.N.Y.Art.	Died	Feb.1814
Woolever, Jacob	Private	15th Inf.	"	12-19-13
Woolf, Amos	Private	15th Inf.	"	
Woolfolk, John H.	Captain	Constitution	Killed	1-22-13
Woolworth, William	Private	13th Inf.	Died	3-15-14
Wooster, Hiram		Champ. Squad.	Killed	9-11-14
Wooten, John	Major		"	
Worden, John	Private	6th Inf.	Died	4-27-13
Worden, Walter	Captain	N.Y. Vols,	Killed	9-20-14
Wyatt, John R.	Private	11th Inf.	Died	12-7-13
Wyer, David	Private	9th Inf.	"	8-15-14
Wyer, William	Sailmaker - Saratoga		Killed	9-11-14
Wyman, Adam	Ensign	8th Reg.Ky.Mil.	Died	Nov.1813
Wright, James	Private	Art.	"	2-26-15
Wright, Jesse	Private	9th Inf.	"	11-23-13
Wright, Jonah	Private	25th Inf.	"	5-10-13
Wright, Judah	Sgt.	25th Inf.	"	11-1-14
Wright, Moses	Private	Co. Art.	"	10-20-14
Wright, Wm.	Private	6th Inf.	"	1-19-14
Yairdly, Richard	Private	12th Inf.	"	1-2-13
Yarborough, Elisha	Private	8th Inf.	"	8-27-14
Yates, James	Private	29th Inf.	"	8-14-14
Yates, James	Private	Ky. Mil.	"	8-16-13
Yates,	Lieut.		Killed	In Battle at Ft. Erie
Yates, John	Private	7th Inf.	Died	4-16-14
Yates, Robert N.	2nd Lt.	4th Rifles	Killed	8-22-14
Yearns, Aquilla	Private	Ky. Inf.	Died	10-1-14
Yeatman, William	Private	Art.	"	10-1-12
Yohn, John	Private	5th Inf.	"	
Yordy, Jacob	Private	22nd Inf.	"	4-29-14
York, Aquilla	Private	Ky. Mil.	"	8-4-13
Young, Alton	Private	45th Inf.	"	10-18-14
Young, Ephraim	Private		"	8-10-13 Quebec Prison
Young, J.	Private	1st Rifles	"	
Young, John	Private	1st Lt. Drag.	"	1-16-14
Young, Nathl.	Private	25th Inf.	"	11-16-14
Young, William		N.C.	"	1-21-14 Dartmoor Prison
Young, Wm.			"	1-21-15 Dartmoor Prison
Younger, Wm.	Private	9th Inf.	"	12-25-13
Younglove, Aaron	Private	29th Inf.	"	9-20-14
Yowell, Humphrey	Private	12th Inf.	"	1-1-14
Zigler, Christian	Private	3rd Inf.	"	1-12-12

SUPPLEMENTARY LIST

Barrows, John		Died	12-31-12	In Maine
Curtis, David		"	1-7-13	" "
Davis, James		"	1-7-13	" "
Freelove, Barney		"	12-31-12	" "
Goodenow, Ezekiel		"	12-3-12	" "
Hamilton, John	Private 12th Inf.	"	7-21-14	
Hewes, Daniel		"	12-31-12	In Maine
Hight, Isaac		"	1-7-13	" "
Hughes, Elias		"	2-12-13	
Hull, Warner		"	12-31-12	In Maine
Norton, Asa		"	1-7-13	" "
Roberts, George		"	1812	" "
Sloan, Sylvanus		"	1-28-13	" "
Smith, Alexander		"	3-4-13	" "
Smith, Alexander		"	2-4-13	" "
Smith, Benjamin		"	12-31-12	" "
Vanderward, Cornelius		"	1-7-13	" "
Weeks, Daniel		"	1815	" "

www.ingramcontent.com/pod-product-compliance
Lightning Source LLC
Chambersburg PA
CBHW031132020426
42333CB00012B/345